ARTHUR C. DANTO

Introduction by Marion Boulton Stroud

ARTHUR C. DANTO

Remarks on Art and Philosophy

Acadia Summer Arts Program

CONTENTS

PIECES OF THOUGHT: ARTHUR DANTO AT A.S.A.P.

MARION BOULTON STROUD

Arthur C. Danto was a monumental, vital presence at Acadia Summer Arts Program, where he presented thirteen annual lectures from 1997 to 2009. He was a figure brimming with life, and his *joie de vivre* was infectious. One felt a better person for knowing him. From the first summer he arrived on Mount Desert Island, he magnanimously extended himself to all the guests in the program through his probing curiosity and enthusiastic interest in everyone's ideas, projects, work and professions. "Oh, how marvelous!" was one of his frequent responses upon hearing of others' plans and proposals. Yet that rejoinder was also the perfect embodiment of him—for how *marvelous* a person Arthur truly was had much to do with his singular capacity to make people feel special and unique. He was a gifted listener, and his benevolent spirit, along with his wit, made for ongoing, memorable conversations and exchanges at A.S.A.P., and sometimes, if you were lucky, a long-lasting friendship.

Arthur's virtuosity as a lecturer was remarkable. His lectures were marked by his brilliance, and by his decades of reflecting upon the meanings of art. They were infused, as well, with a distinct style that included an inimitable repertoire of physical gestures. As events, they were enacted like theater. Like a great Italian baritone, Arthur was a highly animated performer. His hands periodically opened and closed to emphasize a point, or swung in upwards motion before one of them settled on his chin; his eyes looked downward slowly as he pondered and then moved on to his next sentence. Within the lecture room at A.S.A.P. where he sat, nearly always dressed in black, those gesticulations became all the more dramatic, his hands and face accentuated by the light. There on that stage, Arthur became the consummate image of the philosopher that he was—a Rembrandtesque figure emerging from a darkened field. The vibrancy of his intellect was unmistakable. This image was further enlivened by the lyrical structure and cadence of his lecturing style.

Arthur never used slides in any of his talks at A.S.A.P., and very few illustrations appear in his books or his columns for *The Nation*. When asked about this, he responded that showing slides is what art historians do, and that he, by contrast, hardly ever talked about pictures *per se*. Besides, he could safely assume that the audiences at A.S.A.P. were already familiar with the few images to which he referred.

At the beginning of each of his lectures, Arthur always noted the distinction between his two métiers, as he called them—his vocation as a professor of philosophy at Columbia University, where he taught from 1951 until 1992, and his more recent role as the art critic for *The Nation*, a position he assumed in 1984 and maintained for two and a half decades. (It was a longer run than that of most of his predecessors at the magazine.) While he jokingly stated in the first of his talks in Maine that "when I was setting out to be a philosopher, aesthetics was not something . . . that real men were supposed to do," and he subsequently made his mark in analytical philosophy, he nonetheless felt that there was "a real and a deep connection between art criticism and philosophy." Arthur might have found aesthetics to be "incredibly dull" while he was a student, but in his practice of philosophy he found significant crossovers between his chosen field and his later writing about art. In fact, he had studied art and art history in college, and early on he had intended to become an artist. He took up printmaking and exhibited his woodcuts nationally until 1960. (Most of his prints are in a quasi-Abstract Expressionist mode, the reigning style of the period. They were seen at the Art Institute of Chicago, the National Gallery of Art, and elsewhere.) In New York, during his graduate studies at Columbia and his years teaching there, he visited the galleries often, and "fell in" with practicing artists with whom he had extended discussions about art.

Yet it took a certain epiphany to make the connections between art and philosophy tangible and real. One of the recurring themes that he addressed in his lectures at A.S.A.P. was the startling experience of encountering Andy Warhol's *Brillo Boxes* at the Stable Gallery in 1964, and his immediate realization that he "finally knew how it might be possible to do the philosophy of art." As he recounted, he instantaneously saw there was no perceptual distinction between Warhol's replications of the Brillo boxes and the actual commercial shipping cartons. That led him to the question of how Warhol's *Brillo Boxes* could be considered works of art. Aesthetics, Arthur thought, "had nothing to do with it," a huge relief given his initial reservations about the field. To him, it was a matter of when a work of art enters a historic moment in time: the *Brillo Box* could only have happened when it did.

He found Warhol's strategy of replication to be particularly ingenious, as he sensed that art had been liberated from the modernist expectation that it be original, or that it remain centered in the radical renewal of form. For contemporary art after Warhol, as he saw it, all possibilities were open. He described the situation as "anything goes" and found it "liberating."

As a result of his experience of the *Brillo Boxes*, when he began writing about art for *The Nation* in 1984, Arthur also felt freed from the legacy of his predecessors at the journal, such as Clement Greenberg. Unlike them, he felt that he could dispense with an agenda and also refrain from judging a work of art. "Not having an agenda," he stated, "means that to write criticism is not really necessarily to think about how this does or doesn't fit a scheme of art, but how can I find a piece of thought for the object that I'm writing about." As he observed, there ceased to be any single direction or predominant view in art after the 1960s. Many of Arthur's talks at A.S.A.P., however, continued to engage the nagging issue of the use of beauty as a philosophical concept— whether it held any currency, and how he could rethink it as an interpretative strategy. He wondered, for instance, in a number of his lectures—most of which relate to his many books, such as *The Abuse of Beauty*—whether the revival of beauty as a subject in the 1990s by his fellow art critic, Dave Hickey, as well as various art historians and curators, was actually relevant. He concluded in one unforgettable talk in 2004 that he did not "think aesthetics has been the point and purpose of art for most of its history." Rather, as he saw it, the problem was that "the spectrum of the language that is used to characterize something aesthetically" had become too narrow, too preoccupied with the forms and materials of art. Instead, he queried, what about reflecting on both the internal and external meanings of art? That way, any formalist agenda drops by the wayside.

Arthur had the rare ability to distill his abstract ideas and musings on art into highly lucid, elegant and forthright language, his extemporaneous delivery enhanced by his incisive speaking manner and humorous asides. One summer, standing in our office in the midst of the manic pace of activity at A.S.A.P., he pondered on the life and fate of the teeming local insect population and shot off the quip, "when you are a mosquito, every second counts," a light-hearted but razor-sharp observation. For Arthur, if not every second, it seemed that every hour, every day and every year certainly counted, as he never ceased developing his extraordinary body of work that ranges, with equal distinction, from his teaching and his scores of philosophical articles and many books written for his colleagues in the academic world to his art criticism that, when collected, fills multiple volumes and reveals his rare ability to fascinate, stimulate and provoke a broad public. Before his recent death, he was enthusiastic at the prospect of publication of his A.S.A.P. lectures, which touch on many aspects of his life's work (he also curated a number of exhibitions), and underline his importance as a public presence in diverse realms. We will always be grateful to Arthur at A.S.A.P. for his *bons mots*, his warmth of character, the pleasure of his company, and most of all for his dazzling lectures.

A.S.A.P., THE ART WORLD, AND MOUNT DESERT ISLAND

ARTHUR C. DANTO
2005

In the summer months of each year, from late June through mid-September, a certain number of artists, curators, critics and other members of the art world are invited to Mount Desert Island off the coast of Maine, for a period that is theirs to allocate between creation and recreation, in a site of great maritime beauty—of mountains and pine forests, salt air and rockbound waters, sea life and stunning vistas, the cries of gulls and (not to be entirely swept into rhapsody) the nudging whine of mosquitoes—with like-minded persons from the same world as they. The host institution is called A.S.A.P.— the Acadia Summer Arts Program—and it is unique in having no agenda of its own beyond enabling those who attend it to spend their time as they see fit, in the company of others who share their values and hopes, and the belief that art in its nature serves the common good.

The acronym A.S.A.P. has, in current usage, a peremptory edge, meaning, as everyone knows, "as soon as possible." The implied urgency inflects the roster of issued invitations. There are many art worlds, but the one of interest to A.S.A.P. is the international cutting-edge art world, whose members are in one capacity or other engaged with what is happening right now in art. It is an art world of frontiers. Whatever their place in this art world, whether as writers, museum professionals or artists, those invited to A.S.A.P. are mainly among those through whom the concept of art is being extended and tested in an abiding spirit of experimentation and reconfiguration. Part of what makes the A.S.A.P. experience so intoxicating is the combination of a setting of timeless natural beauty with an extreme contemporaneity in its artistic preoccupations.

As a philosopher, I have been engaged for several decades with the concept of the art world and the definition of art. I was recently somewhat shocked to discover that the expression "art world," which I assumed that readers of my opening paragraphs would understand as a matter of course, is not recognized in the *American Heritage Dictionary of the English Language* that comes bundled in with my browser. "Sorry," it said. "We have no matches for *art world*. Did you mean *afterworld*?" I certainly did *not* mean "afterworld" though I would not mind an afterlife in the art world, by contrast with the usual alternatives. But it seemed outrageous that a term that everyone I know uses frequently and spontaneously has so far not been acknowledged as part of the language. Nor could I find it in *Merriam-Webster Online,* included as a "tool" with Internet Explorer. My curiosity piqued, I turned to the lexicographic authority of the 2005 unabridged *Oxford English Dictionary On Line,* where it is listed under sense 18 of the word "art," which also cites its earliest appearance in print. The January 1890 issue of the *Atlantic Monthly* referred to "the culmination of a new movement in the *art world* of Paris."

One thing leads to another when one begins to read the dictionary. Sense 18 of the word "art," used attributively in such compounds as "art appreciation," "art critic" or "art collection," derives, the *OED* holds, from sense 6 "which is the most usual modern sense of art, when used without qualification." This sense is defined as follows: "The skilful production of the beautiful in visible forms." By that definition, what most members of the art world one would encounter at A.S.A.P. would consider art today is not art at all, nor are most of those they consider important artists today really artists, so little does what they produce have to do with "the beautiful in visible forms." But sure enough, "artist" in sense 7c is "One who seeks to express the beautiful in visible forms"—though the lexicographer in charge adds: "popularly, and in the most usual current acceptation of the word, restricted to one who cultivates the art of painting as a profession." When it comes to art, the *Oxford Unabridged Dictionary,* copyright 2005, is in an Edwardian time warp. For what it's worth, the *Grove Dictionary of Art On Line* has no entry for "art world," so I was spared seeing what its editors imagined the definition of art to be. The *Encyclopedia of Aesthetics* does have an article on "Art world," which refers, among others, to me.

Philosophers, even philosophers of art, do not ordinarily count as members of the art world, so it may seem odd that "art world" should merit an article in a philosophical but not in an art historical encyclopedia. It is there not just because the definition of art has been a philosophical problem nearly since the beginning of philosophy itself, but mainly because the concept of art began to change so radically in recent decades that it has little connection with the concept as defined in the *OED,* though a great deal to do with the kind of art with which those at A.S.A.P. are engaged as a matter of course. Philosophers realized that a definition of art that could not explain why Duchamp's readymades—or Andy Warhol's *Brillo Boxes*—were works of art, was badly deficient. A widely discussed effort came to be known as the Institutional Theory of Art, which, crudely speaking, held that something is a work of art if the art world declares it to be one—that what art is, is what the art world says it is. Critics of the Institutional Theory felt it must be obviously wrong. One such critic, the philosopher Richard Wollheim, asked, "Is there really such a thing as the art world, with the coherence of a social group, capable of having representatives, who are in turn capable of carrying out acts that society is bound to endorse?" When and where do they meet, he wondered. Are records kept of their proceedings? Is the art world like the electoral college? Did Warhol's *Brillo Box* get to be a work of art by some overwhelming majority?

It struck me that those questions about the boundaries of art today set the implicit agenda of the growing segment of the art world that finds itself as summer guests of A.S.A.P. It would be a caricature of A.S.A.P. life to see it as a running seminar, a kind of constitutional convention, a forum for determining what is art and what is not. But the life of A.S.A.P. is in fact a benign continuing discourse on what gives meaning and substance to the work and thought of those who listen to one another talk briefly about their work after the community dinners held several times a week, or converse with one another during the dinners or after the talks, or sitting on rocks at lobster picnics—or on the deck of the boat that carries them back and forth from Northeast Harbor to one or another of the nearby islands, or walking through the woods that lead to the pounding surf on the far sides of these empty or sparsely settled islands, past picturesque graveyards or abandoned weathered buildings, or visiting one another's studios when there are no scheduled group events to bring everyone together. The life of art in the world today is what bonds those who come to A.S.A.P. from all parts of the country, and from Europe and Asia and Africa, to share their ideas and experiences, leaving everyone stimulated and enriched, creating memories and friendships, and refreshing the spirit for the return to its normal habitat.

A.S.A.P. is a visionary community, generously conceived, an evolving improvisational fusion of art and life, a tonic for the soul and a shaping force for thought and the enactment of thought. I know nothing to match it in reality and only one concept that comes close to it in literature—the celebrated ideal community envisioned in the sixteenth century by François Rabelais in his masterpiece *Gargantua and Pantegruel*, in which Gargantua establishes an enclave of freedom formed on principles unheard of in the late Middle Ages. This was the Abbaye de Thélème, in which men and women were governed not by laws, rules, or statutes, but only by their good will and freedom of choice. Its single principle was: "Do what you will"—*Fay ce que voudras*. Living under that Golden Rule, life among the Thelemites is sweet, and relationships between them are modulated by courtesy and consideration. No one either at Thélème or A.S.A.P. is required to do anything other than what they want to do, which presupposes the kind of projects creative people always have. But beyond that, opportunities to be with others driven by the same ideals have been put in place, and Mount Desert itself offers untold avenues of exploration.

When they left the Abbaye for whatever reason, the Thelemites must have been a leaven in their society. Often, Rabelais writes, they married one another, largely in order to be with those who had internalized the life of freedom and dedication that prevailed within its charmed walls. Those invited to A.S.A.P. typically bring their significant others along, as well as their children and pets (within reason). It is not an enclave of seclusion, like an art colony. But everyone I know who has participated in A.S.A.P. at all, for any length of time, for a single season or several, has been touched and transformed by the experience. It is a community not merely in the period during which its members reside within the life created in its name, but afterward and forever. I feel blessed in having been afforded a glimpse of the highest possibilities of an enlightened community, and I hope the freedom, light and openness of the weeks spent on Mount Desert, in so exemplary and original a company, have seasoned the writing I have done there and are somehow communicated between the words and the lines to those who have read them.

1997

I'm Arthur Danto, and most people here know me as an art critic. I've been writing for *The Nation* magazine for about thirteen years, writing the column on art. But my basic identity is as a philosopher. I have been for a very long time a professor of philosophy at Columbia University. I think the things that I worked out as a philosopher have largely affected the way in which I write art criticism, and I'll talk a little bit about that. My career in philosophy was not a career in aesthetics at all. For one thing, when I was setting out to be a philosopher, aesthetics was not something, as it were, real men were supposed to do. You had to make your mark as a logician, or as somebody who's interested in logical theory or analytical philosophy, or something fairly severe. And I really enjoyed that kind of philosophy. Moreover, aesthetics as a subject seemed to me incredibly dull. I knew a lot of painters in New York. I just fell in with painters—people like Joe Stefanelli and Wolf Kahn and Joan Mitchell and a number of others—and participated in the discussions that they had, which chiefly had to do with figure and abstraction. These were far more severe than anything I've seen by way of art world discussions since. That period was like the Byzantine empire, and those discussions were really theological, and if they could have burned one another at the stake they would have done it. But I see very little of that idea of stamping out heresy in the art world today.

In 1964 I had a powerful experience with Andy Warhol's work, and that made the discussions of the 1950s seem to me entirely irrelevant to what had happened. Warhol has been a constant source of philosophical as well as critical inspiration, although I never met him. There would have been some awkwardness if I were to have said, "Well, listen, I'm a philosopher, and I think you're just the most interesting artist around." He would have said, "Oh yeah," and "Okay," and we could not have had a discussion.

What interested me about Warhol came up vividly in the first exhibition of his I saw, when his *Brillo Boxes* were shown at the Stable Gallery. When I saw the *Brillo Boxes*, I finally knew how it might be possible to do the philosophy of art. That exhibition opened up two sets of questions which I thought were extremely profound. The first one was that, finally, a work of art had come about which was perceptually indistinguishable, really, from an ordinary object, if you think of the Brillo box in a supermarket as an ordinary object. Hence, the difference between them can't be perceptual. And if it can't be perceptual, then of course you couldn't define art in perceptual terms at all. What you had to do is ask the question a different way, namely, how can this be a work of art and this not be a work of art, if they look exactly alike?

I once had the idea of making a movie called *War and Peace.* It was inspired by Warhol's *Empire,* and it consists of eight hours of footage of the title page of *War and Peace.* Nothing happens in my movie, the page just keeps being that page. You wait for something to happen—but that's it. Imagine two screens side by side, one a moving picture, one a still picture, but nothing visually to tell you there is a difference between them. The Whitney had an exhibition of Warhol's films last year, and I had this wonderful confirmation. I went to see it, of course, because I really love to sit through a certain distance of *Empire* when I get a shot at it, and some guy was sitting there, and then after half an hour he said, "When's the film supposed to begin?" That film had been running for half an hour, but it was as though there were just a very good slide projected on the screen.

I think a subject gets interesting philosophically when you've got two things that are momentously different but can't be told apart. What made the *Brillo Box* a work of art when the Brillo carton wasn't a work of art? (Though the Brillo carton was designed by an artist.) Aesthetics has nothing to do with it, because the aesthetics that you're responding to when you look at Warhol's box is what you would be responding to in the original, the one that was actually designed by James Harvey, who died not very long after the Warhol *Brillo Boxes* were shown.

That was one question, and a book of mine called *The Transfiguration of the Commonplace* [1981] took that question up. The other question was, well, why did it have to happen now? Why couldn't a case like the Brillo box have come up at some earlier time? That led me into some reflections on the philosophy of art history. I tried to form, on the basis of those kinds of questions, a philosophy of art history which would explain things like that. And that was published in my recent book called *After the End of Art* [1997], which culminates in the present moment. But not everybody's a philosopher, so not everybody has the advantage of seeing the show at the Stable Gallery from the angle that I did. I have a friend, a very romantic artist, almost a nineteenth-century man. He said, "You know what I wrote in the guest book? I wrote 'Shit.'" And I said, "You know, the difference between artists and philosophers is, you wrote 'Shit,' and I wrote *The Transfiguration of the Commonplace*." [*laughter*]

One consequence, it seemed to me, of the *Brillo Box* is that if it's a work of art, then anything can be a work of art. Warhol had brought art and reality to such a point that it's only a matter of ingenuity to try and think of circumstances under which any masterpiece and something identical to it could have come into existence, under conditions in which one would and the other wouldn't have been a work of art. I invented a thought experiment in *The Transfiguration of the Commonplace* in which somebody throws a lot of paint and varnish and oil into a centrifuge and gives it a spin and it splats against a wall, and it looks exactly like the *Polish Rider* of Rembrandt. There it is—the rider, riding toward what? His death? Who knows? But, a splat— that wouldn't have the moral meaning of the *Polish Rider*. So I thought from now on, anything really can go, and that was an extremely liberating idea, confirmed, it seems to me, by what has happened in the art world. That is to say, there is no longer any heresy; we're living in a state of almost complete pluralism. That's the deep structure of the present moment. There's a great advantage to that freedom. At the moment, for instance, one of the things I'm deeply interested in is the structure of exhibitions. There's a transformation in the art world, through the emergence of the curator, who organizes exhibitions. I thought about a sentence from the logician Frege, who says that a word has meaning only in the *zusammenhang* of a sentence—only in the context of a sentence. And I thought maybe only in the context of an exhibition does a painting have meaning. I think that meanings are now being elicited of a kind nobody knew was there, through the idea of an exhibition.

All this affects the way in which I do art criticism—that is, to have no agenda. As a philosopher, you don't get hooked into agendas, into ideologies. I've got certain things that I like a lot, but I couldn't be a critic if I went by what I like. Certain things come along that make me think to myself, "Oh, Christ, am I going to have to deal with this?" But I put out, you know, I make the effort, and I deal with it. I think that being a philosopher—somebody who's not dependent on the art world in any way—is a very good position to be in. There's no way in which I could have an agenda—unlike, I think, most of my predecessors. *The Nation* is a very old magazine. *The Nation* was founded in July 1865. They had art criticism in *The Nation* right from the start. I got interested in my predecessors there. Henry James—I mean, talk about a predecessor—wrote art criticism for *The Nation* starting around 1867. And in 1873—I was just reading this a few weeks ago—his mother writes that he had received five checks from *The Nation*. They totaled $250. James was able to live in Rome for $14 a week, room and board and horseback, and so forth. Clement Greenberg was art critic there from 1942 to 1949, and Fairfield Porter from 1949 to 1951. Hilton Kramer, if you can believe it, wrote for *The Nation*, for a period at any rate, when his political principles were a little different from what they are today. And Max Kozloff. Then before me was Lawrence Alloway, and I think all those people had pretty strong agendas, pretty strong ideas as to what art is supposed to be. I have pretty strong ideas about that too, in the sense that there is no way art's supposed to be any longer. There's no way of generating an agenda, except at the most abstract level, or a definition of art at the most abstract level, that's going to do justice to all the different kinds of things that are happening now.

Not having an agenda means that to write criticism is not necessarily to think about how a work does or doesn't fit a scheme of art, but rather, how can I find a piece of thought for the object that I'm writing about. Usually the thought comes out somewhat philosophically. The idea of a piece of thought is Duchamp's, in a way. Duchamp said, in the issue of *The Blind Man* [May 1917] where he wrote about his notorious readymade, the porcelain urinal titled *Fountain* and pseudonymously signed "R. Mutt," that Mr. Mutt "CHOSE it . . . and created a new thought for that object." I approach an art exhibition in such a way that the people who read the review can check it out against their own observations, because I have a tacit contract with the readers of *The Nation* that they'll be able to see whatever show I write about. I mean, geography permitting. My reviews don't come out afterwards, the way they do in most art magazines, for example, and I have a little bit more time to think than the daily papers give writers. I want the reviews to be deep enough that when people go, they can say, "Well, I don't know what got into Danto," and so forth and so on. But there's a worked-out theory. It's not an art magazine, *The Nation*, even though, as I say, it's always had art criticism, and it is read mainly by people who are fairly intelligent people. I've never had the editor say to me, "Oh, our readers won't know what you're trying to say. You're going to have to simplify." I once, just to see what would happen, put in a paragraph of Latin. I was reviewing a show of Sofonisba Anguissola and there was a Latin inscription on a painting of hers, so I said what the hell, and just did it. I never even got a letter from anybody saying, "Who the hell do you think you are? Remember the proletariat." I mean it's a fairly left-wing magazine, but the editors feel, "Yeah, our readers. Latin? Okay." They treat the readers with dignity, and it's a great place to write for that reason. *The Nation*'s readers don't know the art world, most of them, but people from the art world do read that column, too. I try to think in terms of what the readers of *The Nation* would be interested in if they were to make a special trip from wherever they come from.

In writing art criticism it helps, I think, to be a philosopher, and it helps not to be an art historian. A really interesting history could be written about the successive waves of art critics in the United States. The first professional critics were at *The Nation* and the *New York Herald*, and for a long time, a fairly long time, you had journalists whose beat was art. It was nice to be an art critic because it gave you opportunity for jocularity, especially once the avant garde came on the scene in 1913 with *Nude Descending a Staircase*. After the journalists, the poets began to write about art, in *ARTnews* and elsewhere—Frank O'Hara and John Ashbery, then Peter Schjeldahl, Bill Berkson, Carter Ratcliff, and others. And the poets were far more advocates, far less jocular at the expense of the artists. Then art historians came to the forefront, and articles began to grow footnotes, lengthy, lengthy footnotes, particularly when *Artforum* became a central publication. They had a scholarly point of view, and art criticism and art history were very close. Then there was a moment when some artists wrote wonderful art criticism. They were extremely intelligent people—the ones best able to talk about their art. Donald Judd would have been one, and of course he had been a working critic for many years. Another would have been Robert Morris, and Robert Smithson and Mel Bochner would have been two more. After that, you had intellectuals who wanted to be art philosophers, but didn't know how to be. That is to say, the footnotes would begin to have Baudrillard or Derrida in them, or one or another continental import. And now it's the philosophers' turn to practice art criticism in probably the most heterogeneous art world that's ever existed.

The thing about the *Brillo Box* is that it played into a preexisting piece of philosophical structure that's actually been around since Platonic times. For example, Descartes begins with the following problem: how do I know I'm not dreaming, since my experience could be the same whether I were dreaming it or experiencing it? You've got illusion and real experience, and they're exactly alike, and there's no internal criteria by which you could tell the difference, and yet the difference is momentous. That's where philosophy begins. But when you start dealing with other kinds of artwork, you can't that easily graft it onto a piece of preexisting philosophical structure. You're dealing here with a human product and you really try to see what makes it work. And that's about all I ever do as a critic. I mean, I'm not terribly negative, although I have been sometimes, but usually on moral grounds, to be candid. That is to say, there have been instances when I felt that the viewer was being treated in a shabby way by the artist. But in the main, I think if you can answer two questions—these questions really were articulated by Hegel—what's it about— what's the content—and how does it embody that content, you've probably gone as far as anybody knows how to go. Taste has nothing to do with it, as far as I'm concerned, because tastes are beside the point. That was not always true. Greenberg, certainly, and Kramer prided themselves on their good taste. I think that taste is an extremely private thing, and I wouldn't want it out there. But I love the idea of dealing with something where I can, first of all, see what it's about, and then how it embodies that about-ness, so you've got content and you've got material. And then after all, I only get two thousand words, and that's about as much as I want. Thank you.

1998

I'm Arthur Danto and I've been the regular art critic for *The Nation* magazine since 1984. Along with that, I've been a professor—was a professor of philosophy at Columbia University. I'm convinced that there's a real and a deep connection between art criticism and philosophy, but there probably aren't enough philosophers who are also art critics or vice versa to test a theory of any sort. Notwithstanding which, I see the two as rather deeply related. What I really want to talk about this evening in the minutes allotted me is something which is neither philosophy nor art criticism, but an exhibition I curated in which something like art criticism and philosophy played a role.

There was a wonderful talk the other evening here by Amada Cruz about her show—her and Elizabeth Smith's show—of Cindy Sherman [in 1997 at the Chicago Museum of Contemporary Art]. There was a piece that Cindy was commissioned to do by the magazine *Artforum*. And characteristically of Cindy's mind, she decided to do it as a centerfold, which has that aura of Eros. Amada showed it, and according to Cindy's narrative of that figure, it was meant to represent a Manhattan sophisticate, a young single Manhattan girl or woman who spent the night dancing and has come back, her makeup in disarray, her hair disheveled, and she's collapsed in bed. *Artforum*, in the end, did not publish it. And the reason was that they saw a very different narrative, they saw that she had just been raped. The question struck me, how would you ever tell which of the two narratives was the correct one? That seemed to me to connect with two questions that interest me as a critic and as a philosopher. The critical part was, could you do a piece of art criticism that would disambiguate the work, if there really were two narratives? That is to say, thinking of a piece of art criticism as inferring to the best explanation of why things look the way they look, could you apply a piece of art criticism so you can say, no, it's really just what Cindy wants it to be, a Manhattan woman, a Bacchante, or is it that the people at *Artforum* are right? As a problem, if I were teaching a class on art criticism—which I've never done—then I'd say, all right, here are these two narratives. Which is the right, which is the true one?

It doesn't necessarily mean that you'd get a correct answer or a satisfying answer. You'd probably have to do a fair amount of negotiating over the evidence, but that question is connected to a question that has been of great interest to me in the philosophy of language, namely about the limits of picturability: what are the limits of what you can show as over and against what you can say? I'm thinking of a very simple kind of case—certainly not the logically sublime kinds of cases that Wittgenstein talks about—where the artist undertakes to represent pictorially non-visual qualities which are supposed to explain what you see in the picture. That got to be a very important problem for artists until the pictorial tradition more or less disappeared, because most artists were involved in showing narratives. To show a narrative means that you have to give enough visual evidence so that people will be able to infer to the best explanation of what they see. For example, in Giotto's great painting of Christ raising Lazarus from the grave, you see Christ and you see other people and you see Lazarus bound up in the grave clothes, but there are two people standing next to Lazarus, and they're holding their noses. That's a strange thing to find in a painting. It almost seems inconsistent with the awesomeness of the miracle that Giotto is depicting. But it's in the Bible. When Christ comes to Bethany, he comes too late to be at Lazarus's side. He says, "Take me to the grave," and Martha, Lazarus's sister, says, "My Lord, he has been dead for four days, he stinketh. He stinketh." I love the Bible with that rich grasp of Palestinian reality. I mean, that's what happens to bodies when they've lain there. And yet, forensically, it's the best evidence you've got that Lazarus really was dead, that is to say, it wasn't a hoax of any kind. And I started following the history of the nose holders, and they went so far back that I even found one in the tenth century, a sculpture where Lazarus is sitting up, holding his own nose. Later, that dies out, and when you get to Caravaggio there are no nose holders. Lazarus has got rigor mortis, which was Caravaggio's way of handling the subject. Those examples, at any rate, are what I mean by pictorial intelligence, which picture makers had to deal with in the Renaissance and really throughout the history of painting.

And now I want to talk a little bit about this exhibition I organized. I was invited by Gunnar Kvaran, the director of the Rasmus Meyer Museum in Bergen, Norway, who's become a pal. He'd just taken over as the director, and he asked if I would come and curate a show out of their permanent collection. I almost always say yes to questions like that—I'll more or less do anything that comes along if it seems like it's going to be interesting. His idea was that the most interesting thing about that particular museum was its permanent collection, so why not get somebody to do an exhibition out of the collection? There are about 5,000 pieces in the collection. You can make many exhibitions out of a finite number of pieces. If you've got a study collection of ten pieces, you'll get 3,628,000 different permutations. In the museum there were 5,000 pieces, so the possibilities approached a human equivalent of infinity, so where would you begin? It was a wonderful collection in one sense. It had 150 Munchs in it. And you can't go deeply wrong with Munch, but it seemed to me cheating to give Munch a one-man show at this stage. It also seemed to me cheating if I were to say, well, these were my favorite pictures and hang them on the wall. For one thing, I didn't have that many favorite pictures there. I wasn't that interested in the collection, which mostly consisted in nineteenth- and some eighteenth-century Norwegian paintings.

So, the question then was how to bring them all together under a single concept, and narrativity was what finally gripped me. I began to think that everything in the museum, practically—except a few still lifes and a few landscapes—was telling a certain kind of story. And hence, here was an opportunity to get across these preoccupations that I have with narrative intelligence. I was supposed to fill four galleries. I found these very old Italian paintings from the thirteenth century of the Annunciation and the Madonna and Child. I thought, these are stories everybody knows, you don't have to put a lot of intelligence into those pictures because everybody will know that it's the Annunciation, everybody will know that it's the Madonna and Child. Those are extremely unambiguous pictures. So in front of each of the first three galleries, there was a kind of wall. I put the Annunciation on one wall and the Madonna and Child next, and then a twentieth-century Norwegian painting of a Crucifixion, so there you got a narrative straight across.

I used the Annunciation to define a class of narratives for the first gallery, and those were narratives almost of epistemology of cognition. I called the first room "Disclosures and Hidden Truths," and I had a Baroque Saint Paul falling off his horse, and Mary Magdalene, who was praying for what happened to Saint Paul to happen to her. All through that gallery there were people who were searching or looking, or messages were being conveyed that had to be eked out, meanings that had to be grasped. There were even a few tricks I put in there. There was one painting of laundry hanging on a line, and I put it in because at the end of *Finnegan's Wake*, the women are doing the laundry and telling stories about all the people who did this and that between the bed sheets, and so forth. I've associated that with narration ever since I read it.

In the second gallery, where the Madonna was, I decided to let that be stages in a human life, the story of lives. I had the woman's life going up one side, the man's life going up the other side. There weren't enough interesting things, oddly enough, in a man's life. The women's lives are a lot more interesting, at least as far as the artists are concerned. I mean, you begin with childhood and maidenhood and meeting the guy and getting Grandma's wedding dress, and then, of course, standing at the grave of your husband, who pre-deceases you. But the male life turned out not to be that interesting. And then, at the back, I put this spectacular Munch of the stages of a woman's life that was quite wonderful and then a Norwegian statue. It was very metaphysical, that one. The restorers had been working on this eighteenth-century Diana and they were deeply disappointed that I wasn't going to use it, so I felt an obligation to find a place for Diana. Barbara [his wife, the artist Barbara Westman] and I had noticed that Munch's paintings, characteristically, operate on two levels. You see a face and then you see what's going on behind the face. As in *Jealousy*, you see this couple and the man has this horrified and tragic face. So I decided, here is Munch's painting of a young woman standing by a bed and obviously discovering—you feel— her body. And I put the Diana next to that painting to suggest what the woman was thinking about, namely, I shall be a virgin for the rest of my life. That's the only association I could get for Diana.

The Crucifixion was the key to the third gallery. And that was, of course, connected with the *Iliad*, with suffering and with warfare. It was a snap to pick out narratives which dealt with those themes. In all these cases, the viewers, if they got involved, were asked—were required, I guess I'd have to say—to try and figure out what was going on in some of these strange paintings. What story were they supposed to get from that? Did the artist succeed in getting that narrative across?

Finally, in the last room I didn't have a wall at the entrance, and at any rate I'd run out of stages in the Christian epic to put in front as an index. I used the idea of a Homeric paradigm of travel, of the trip, of the voyage, and of home. There were a lot of home paintings, and it was clear that home, or the concept of home, meant a lot to the Norwegians. But putting them together with travelers seemed to me to bring out narrative potentialities in the paintings of homes. There, again, I had this wonderful Munch of a woman. If I were titling the painting, I would call it *The First Step*. She's walking out on a jetty, and behind her are these people gossiping in the village, and you feel that it would be a magnificent illustration to Ibsen's *A Doll's House*—that the woman is breaking away and taking that first step.

Anyway, that was the show. When I talked in the gallery, I said it was a postmodern show, essentially. I said if I were a modernist, I couldn't show narratives. It's the kind of topic that you'd be criticized for because it's too literary or it's illustrational or something of that sort. But the nice thing about being a postmodern person is that narrativity is perfectly acceptable now. I couldn't have done a modernist show based upon those paintings— the formalistic considerations were so tertiary that there would be no way in which you could put them together. I'm not sure that my show was the right way to do it, but I can't imagine any other way. Next year the director has asked Alain Robbe-Grillet to do this job. And in the year 2000, Umberto Eco is going to do it. I can't say that I'm enthralled with Bergen, but I would go back just to see what those who follow me can do differently from what I did. Thanks.

1999

I'm Arthur Danto. Most people in this audience will know me as the art critic for *The Nation* magazine, for which I've written a regular column since 1984. I've also been a professor of philosophy at Columbia University for an even longer time. Philosophy has been my main calling and livelihood. Most of you probably remember an essay by Dave Hickey from early in the decade, when he was asked at a conference, "What do you think the main direction"—the *problématique,* as the Europeans say—"of the 1990s is going to be?" And Dave said, "The problem of the 1990s? Beauty. Beauty will be the problem of the 1990s." I don't know whether it was prophetic, but in some sense, the problem of the 1990s does seem to be, in one form or another, the status of beauty. I'm speaking here primarily of the art world, but also of the philosophical world, and in some sense the political world. Since Richard Shiff's conference at the University of Texas at Austin, "Whatever Happened to Beauty?" [1992], hardly a month passes before another anthology on the topic of beauty is announced, or a panel is called, or an issue of a journal gets devoted to beauty. It's my destiny to be called upon in connection with most of these things, not out of any inclination on my part, but because I do have a philosophical background and might be expected to know something about beauty, which has a long philosophical tradition.

In October, there's going to be an exhibition at the Hirshhorn Museum, curated by Neal Benezra and Olga Viso, and it's called "Regarding Beauty." I have no clear idea of what will be in the show or what particularly motivated them, but I am preparing an essay for the catalogue. One of the things that deeply interested me is that the same two curators, two years ago, put on a show called "Distemper: Dissonant Themes in Contemporary Art," and if you were someone who watched the zeitgeist, you'd say, well, history doesn't usually turn on a dime, but two years from dissonance to a show regarding beauty gives the impression of some kind of sharp curve that the spirit of the times has taken.

It's the kind of thing that I think would encourage the organizers of a conference I attended at the University of Chicago, sponsored by the archconservative Olin Foundation, thinking, as many conservatives do, that hostility to beauty has been a long aberration, and here all at once beauty seems to be back. Well, that would probably be the wrong message for somebody to get, if you think, for example, of two artists who caused the greatest ruckus in the history of American subsidization to the arts, Robert Mapplethorpe and Andres Serrano—both of them profoundly interested in beauty. Mapplethorpe, on whom I once wrote a book, said that in fact, all he was interested in was beauty. I think he was an artist whose work could be described as beautiful. But it got him in hot water, not only because of the content, which was a ready target for hostile politicians, but because of the beauty, with many people in the art world fairly turned off by the beauty. The general tendency on the part of people who subscribe to a materialist aesthetic of what photographs should be would've thought that Mapplethorpe was on a tangent—that he was out of phase, out of date.

Here we are at the end of the century, at the end of the millennium, and I would be hard-pressed to find a text on the subject of beauty, a philosophical text, for example, that comes to very much. When I was a graduate student, which was in the period of high positivism, all philosophical problems were turned into linguistic problems, and from asking what is the definition of beauty, people would say, "Well, when would I say that's beautiful?" The answer was, you don't say it when you want to describe something. You say it when you want to express a positive attitude toward it. Alanna Heiss, for example, has said "beautiful" here on three occasions in presenting slides. She said, "That's beautiful." But the giveaway is she said twice, "Beautiful, beautiful." And the reiterated "beautiful" in that way is quite clearly an expression of enthusiasm, rather than a description of a work.

So is there anything more to say about beauty than this emotivist idea that it's just a reaction? It's not very different from the way art world people operate. The art world "Wow," for example, is an expression, not a description. It's a civilized way of swooning, you might say, what the Stendhal syndrome entails. You're supposed to be in the presence of beauty and swoon. It's not a description, but a response. Olga tried to find a painting of somebody swooning in front of a painting. It's surprising that they don't exist. *ARTnews*, when it talked about the Stendhal syndrome, had to get a cartoonist to do something. And I thought, given that you could still find painters capable of depicting rapture, that would've been a very romantic theme, but it doesn't exist.

When people do talk about beauty, they're comfortable with saying something like—well, it's all in the eye of the beholder, or it's all in the mind of the beholder. Which was a thought originally ascribed to the philosopher David Hume. The problem is that for Hume, everything was in the mind. That is to say, there was nothing that existed outside the mind. That was the radicalism of Hume's philosophy. You're not saying very much about beauty when you say it's in the eye of the beholder. So are "red" and "smooth" and "wet" and so forth, all those descriptive terms, in the mind of the beholder. I've got this terrific passage that I want to read to you, to get some sense of what a wonderful thinker Hume was. This is in one of Hume's essays ["The Sceptic"]:

> Were I not afraid of appearing too philosophical, I should remind my reader of that famous doctrine, supposed to be fully proved in modern times, "That tastes and colours, and all other sensible qualities, lie not in the bodies, but merely in the senses." The case is the same with beauty and deformity, virtue and vice. This doctrine, however, takes off no more from the reality of the latter qualities than from that of the former; nor need it give any umbrage either to critics or moralists. Though colours were allowed to lie only in the eye, would dyers or painters ever be less regarded or esteemed? There is a sufficient uniformity in the senses and the feelings of mankind, to make all these qualities the objects of art and reasoning, and to have the greatest influence on life and manners. And as it's certain, that the discovery above mentioned in natural philosophy makes no alteration in action and conduct, why should a like discovery in moral philosophy make any alteration?

I thought that was a magnificent way of thinking about beauty—that you compare it to the other senses. In Hume's time, there were people who actually thought there was a sense of beauty. And he has an ingenious argument, which I particularly admire because it brings into the discussion some of what I think of as the structures of art criticism.

So that was a fairly magnificent beginning, which after Hume, I think, never got very far. We move into the twentieth century, as I say, and beauty's not really been much of a topic. It wouldn't seem to be on the front burner of artistic concern today—and yet, there it is. How did it happen that people have not been at all concerned about beauty? My own view, as an amateur art historian, is that it probably must begin with Dada. There are texts by Max Ernst and Hans Arp where they talk about this society which believes in truth, goodness and beauty, and has just sent tens of thousands of young men to die in the World War. So they were going to injure that society in the best way they could, and they were going to make art which was buffoonish, childish— whatever the case, anything but beautiful. I think that what the Dada artists did was to politicize the concept of beauty, but I also think that theirs was the great conceptual breakthrough in the philosophy of beauty in the twentieth century, in the sense that they showed that it was perfectly possible to make art which wasn't beautiful. I don't think anybody from Hume on down had thought of art as something that was as loosely related to beauty as the Dadaists implied it was. I think that got nailed in place with Duchamp and his radically anti-aesthetic attitude, his effort to abolish taste from the work of art, along with the artist's hand, the artist's eye, all those things that connoisseurs prize in works of art. I think he made it fairly clear that, rather than being part of the essence of art, beauty was an option. That was what the Dadaists seemed to me to have demonstrated. And that means, under what circumstances do you want to exercise that option? Why would you want to create beauty, knowing you're not really any longer required to do that? You're no less an artist because the work isn't beautiful.

I have tried to devote my essay for the Hirshhorn catalogue to that particular question. And I can only sketch what I think is a right answer. In a way, it does connect with what I think my practices as an art critic are. What you've got to try to do is to see the work, any work, as a piece of thought. As an art critic, very much like a philosopher, you're concerned with the logical clarification of that thought. What thesis—what idea—is being advanced by means of it, and how does the work manage to advance that thought? As a critic, that, it seems to me, is what you're obliged to do. From that point of view, thinking of works of art as pieces of thought, rather than just as objects, when you find beauty in a work of art, the question is, what does it mean? Not is the object beautiful or not, but what does it mean that it should be beautiful? Is that part of the analysis, and if it is part of the analysis, through what piece of art criticism are you going to explain why it's beautiful?

I won't talk very much longer, but I'll give an example of what I've got in mind. I think Robert Motherwell's "Elegies to the Spanish Republic" are extremely beautiful paintings. He did about 175 of the Elegies, and there are a couple of forms that keep appearing, some ovals and one or two vertical bars, and people have said, "Well, it's a bull's penis and balls." Well, no. I mean, you don't write elegies for a bull's penis and balls. The bull might write some kind of an elegy. [*laughter*] But that can't be; that doesn't go with the elegiac mode. So I think the way to see those works that makes sense of them being called elegies is that these are figures in a devastated landscape. You've got architectural components and you've got human components, and maybe some sand or some red for blood, but mostly it's these black figures moving through burnt timbers. That, at any rate, is the feeling of those forms. At first you say, well, if that's the subject, if that's what they're about—Spain at that time, in the 1930s—why make it beautiful? Isn't there something almost obscene in responding with beauty to that? And then I thought, well, that's what an elegy is supposed to do. I thought about everything that goes with memorializing someone who has died. I thought of funereal practices. People bring flowers, there's music, there are beautiful words. It's a way of coping with irremediable loss. And I thought that beauty is internally connected with the meaning of these paintings being elegies.

I began to look at paintings where it didn't seem to me it was ever controversial whether these were or weren't beautiful paintings. But what did beauty mean in those cases? Something different, it seems to me, from what beauty means when we look at the harbor or we look at the sunrise on Mount Desert Island. That would seem to me then to say, this is how you exercise the option of making a work of art beautiful. You ask yourself, in what way does its being beautiful contribute to the larger meaning of the work? I don't know whether that would operate very easily for the works that Neal and Olga have chosen. I imagine Olga will get a shot at talking about the show when she is here at the camp, later this summer. But it would be the way, if I hadn't written the introduction, I would go in as an art critic thinking about the artists, and whether their creating beauty meant anything or not.

The last thought that I would like to express is, if there's anything to that analysis, then the reason beauty has begun to come forward—and I think you really have to be a historian to understand why in this particular decade beauty has asserted itself in the works, or at least the preoccupations, of curators and artists and others—is that art itself is becoming more spiritual than it has been. I don't mean by spiritual anything particularly religious, but I mean something like this: Hegel, from whom I've borrowed a lot in writing about this subject, is at great pains to distinguish between natural beauty and artistic beauty, and he said artistic beauty is born of the spirit and born again, and that it is essentially a rational operation. You can ask what it's about, you can ask whether it's true or false, whereas that doesn't come up with natural beauty. If the paintings are in the show only in the way in which a bouquet would be in the show, then it doesn't seem to me that the beauty amounts to anything. But if the artists have found things that they want to say, to the saying of which beauty is an essential component, then it seems to me that there is a deep reconnection with a tradition, and people are right in thinking that something fundamental has taken place. Thank you.

2000

I'm Arthur Danto and probably, with this audience, I'm best known for the writings that I do for *The Nation* magazine, where I'm the art critic. But I'm on loan from the world of professional philosophy, and this talk is going to be about art and philosophy. Last year I talked a bit about beauty, and this time I thought I would get into a somewhat more central topic. It won't start sounding like philosophy until about halfway through, but you have to remember I come from a fairly minimalist school of philosophy, so it begins insidiously. I don't have any slides. Philosophers do need some examples, and I find that I get along best with one example that is known to everybody. Namely, the *Brillo Box* of Andy Warhol, which has the distinction of being not only the icon of the movement that it comes from, but has in its own right become a part of popular consciousness. So much so that everybody knows it in the same way in which they know Elvis and Marilyn and Jackie and Liz and the other icons that Warhol is responsible for. And like Warhol himself, who belongs to popular consciousness as the only artist of the twentieth century who is instantly recognized by everybody.

It's the most famous work, in my view—well, at least as famous as the *Mona Lisa,* which Warhol has also popularized. But with the difference that probably more people can identify the artist who did the *Brillo Box* than can tell you the artist who did the *Mona Lisa*. The *Brillo Box* is known all over the world, including most countries where Brillo doesn't exist as a commodity. I know that from my own experience. My French publisher, when they did a book of mine called *Beyond the Brillo Box* [1992], thought that nobody knew what Brillo was in France, and so they gave it a different title. And that gave every critic the opportunity to say what the real title was and what Brillo was. In most other countries they know that people will be a lot more interested in reading about Warhol than they would anything that I myself might say, so they keep the word Brillo in the title, whether Brillo in fact is sold in their country or not. It has also survived the actual carton that Warhol replicates. If you go to a supermarket today and ask to see how Brillo is shipped, you'll see a brown, fairly nondescript cardboard box with Brillo stenciled on it and a piece of plastic at each end to hold the packets of Brillo from getting lost. So something really profound has happened to the culture since 1964, when the Brillo box was, as a matter of fact, used to ship the soap pads. Of the Warhol *Brillo Box* there are perhaps 200 exemplars—he did about that many. And despite the fact that there were countless thousands of commercially produced Brillo cartons in existence, very few of them exist now, so far as I know. I mean, they're in attics and garages and basements, storing things, but you rarely see one. In my whole experience, I only know of two. One of them was found in a dumpster by the artist Mike Bidlo, and he called me with some considerable excitement, that he'd found an original Brillo box. It was like an archaeological treasure to see that. We both, for example, pored over what Warhol never painted, which was the underside of the box. And we were very interested in who actually manufactured it, and issues of that sort.

Now that's one, and the other original Brillo carton belongs to the distinguished art historian Irving Sandler, and it comes with a somewhat interesting story. James Harvey, who was the actual designer of the Brillo box, was also an Abstract Expressionist painter. He had a show at the Graham Gallery in 1961 that was a considerable success. He was reviewed enthusiastically in the *New York Times* by Brian O'Doherty, and the show sold out the next day. When Warhol's *Brillo Boxes* were shown in 1964, the Graham gallery distributed a press release saying how unfair it was that Warhol at the Stable Gallery was selling these boxes for a lot of money, and after all it was James Harvey's work. And Irving twitted Harvey saying, "Well, I'm surprised you would do that to a fellow artist." Harvey replied he had nothing to do with the press release, and then Irving said, "What you should do is sell some of your boxes, maybe 25¢ each, and compete with Andy that way." A few weeks later, Irving told me, a Brillo box arrived in the mail from James Harvey, signed. And today it sits in a protective Plexiglas case, and Irving says it's the last thing he sees at night when he turns out the light.

The *Brillo Box* has entered philosophical discourse largely, I think, through me, since I began to write about it in 1964, originally in a rather austere publication called the *Journal of Philosophy*. But it has been continuously discussed by philosophers who probably don't know any other examples of works of contemporary art. Though rather less, I think, by art historians. It's on my mind at the moment because in December we had a

Brillo Box conference in Nuremberg, which was sponsored by the Akademie der Bildenden Künste, and a very select group of intellectuals and some artists from the United States and Europe convened for a couple of days to discuss the metaphysics, as it were, of the *Brillo Box*. I take a certain pleasure in contemplating the fact that the *Brillo Box* was being discussed in an academy in the same town that Hegel strode the streets of, a long time ago, when he was headmaster of a school, before his own career took off.

I'd like to just talk a bit about my interest in the *Brillo Box*. Because after all, the *Brillo Box* is not like the van Eyck altarpiece. You can't look at it for days on end and keep discovering new truths. It's not the kind of thing in connection with which there's a lot of very relevant scholarship, and everything I've said so far is quite irrelevant except, I think, for the fact that James Harvey was involved. And Harvey is somebody I'm pretty interested in, as a matter of fact. At the present moment I'm contemplating organizing an exhibition of his work. It will be called "Behind the Brillo Box," and it will have as many of his paintings as I can track down. So far I've not had a lot of luck. But my hope is that there will be the paintings and there will be the Brillo box, and art historians can try and think about the influence of Abstract Expressionism on the Brillo box. I like the idea, if possible, of bringing Harvey back from the dead. He died in 1965 a very young man; he was in his thirties and had never had the kind of career that one might have anticipated for him.

My interest in the *Brillo Box* is against the background of a fairly longstanding philosophical question, namely, how do you distinguish art from reality? It is a question which has been around since ancient times. Plato and Aristotle both participated in the early history of the question. And most of what's been said since has been by way of footnotes to Plato and Aristotle. I'll begin with just a word about Aristotle, because he's very familiar; it's not obscure knowledge. He had a theory of art as imitation, but it was a theory, it would be a theory that wouldn't carry you very far in connection with Warhol's *Brillo Box* as over and against Harvey's Brillo box, because you couldn't tell which was the imitation. They look exactly alike. They don't embody, in any way, separately, which is the imitation and which is not. It was a question that wouldn't have come up for Aristotle because he was thinking of obvious kinds of cases, like a statue which would be an imitation of a human being. It would be very rare for a human being to be an imitation of a statue, although I suppose there could be a *tableau vivant,* in which a person poses as the *Discobolus.* But the difference at least is this, that there are possible worlds, as philosophers like to say, in which Harvey's Brillo box could have been an imitation of Warhol's *Brillo Box.* I mean, there could have been Brillo boxes in the real world made out of plywood, and then, using paper, a far more typical artist's material, Harvey could have imitated the wood box that way, in cardboard. On the other hand, there are very few possible worlds in which we could say of a marble statue, "That could be a human being." There are myths, for sure, like the myth of Pygmalion, but for the most part it requires a mythic intervention if marble is to turn to flesh. We're not talking about turning anything into something else, it's just that this could have been the imitation and that the reality, or that the reality and this the imitation. There are differences between the two, but my question was, how can we have two things that look that much alike, when one of them is a work of art and one is just a utilitarian object? That question had never quite been asked before, and when I began to ask it, a lot of people said, "Well, but look, they are different. This is made out of wood; that is made out of paper," et cetera. I said, "You mean the distinction between art and reality depends upon this being paper and that being wood?" That didn't make sense to me. I mean, it's supposed to be a momentous distinction and it wouldn't work that way. There was a certain amount of critical literature based on those kinds of objections, which seemed to me not to amount to much. So for my purposes, think of them as just exactly alike.

In 1964 I could have used other examples, and that connects me to Plato. There were a lot of beds beginning to appear in the art world around that time. Rauschenberg exhibited a bed; it was a bed. It belonged, actually, to Dorothea Rockburne, and there are various stories of how Rauschenberg got his paws on it. There was a really creepy bed by Claes Oldenburg. There was a bed that appeared in an installation by George Segal. So there were plenty of beds around at that time. Beds have a really interesting resonance for people who know the history of philosophy, because they figure in Book 10 of the *Republic,* where Plato tries to say, in effect, there are three kinds of beds. There is the form of the bed and then there are the kinds of beds in which that form participates, which carpenters make and in which you could sleep, and then there are the beds that artists make, which are just imitations and not worth much; from that point of view artists don't have to know anything. Socrates says, holding a mirror up, "Look, anybody can do something like that. I can imitate a bed as well as the best painter in Athens." I thought, well, here we are. It took a couple thousand years but artists are beginning to get promoted in the scale of being. They're actually neck and neck with carpenters. They're using real beds and so forth. Later I thought I could have made the points that I was interested in better with the beds than with the Brillo box, because in the case of Segal he made an artwork out of a real bed. There was no difference between the artwork and the real bed that anybody could point to, nothing palpable.

But I liked the *Brillo Box* for the cheekiness and because art is always supposed to be a fairly tremendous kind of thing in the history of philosophy. I just loved the fact that here was this Brillo box, a piece out of the common culture. And I know now—didn't know at the time—that there were a lot of people around in the art world in New York who were interested in collapsing the distinction between art and life, coming out of Cage's seminar in composition at the New School and out of Fluxus. I didn't know about Fluxus until 1984 when I saw it in an exhibition called "Blam!" at the Whitney Museum, which was the first show I reviewed when I took on the position of critic. The Fluxus artists were interested in Cage's overcoming of the distinction between musical sounds and sounds *tout court*. Why can't we make music out of any sounds? And parallel questions were being taken up by people in dance; Paul Taylor did a dance— again, that I knew nothing about at the time—where he more or less just sat on stage and listened to telephone recordings of the time of day. There was something in the air, you might say, in the early 1960s, and even earlier. Even if I'd known about it, I would have said, "I'm not interested in overcoming the distinction between art and reality, I just want to know how you get art to come out of all this. Because I can see that you can have an artwork that is just like *anything*, as plain and ordinary as you please. So how does it get to be art?"

Well, to make a long story short, I worked at the question for a while and I came up with a couple of thoughts. My first thought was that it's got to be about something. Things aren't about anything but works of art are about something. It's at least legitimate to say, "What's its meaning? What's it about?" So for a certain class of cases I thought the meaning should in some way be embodied; it should be, in some way, recoverable from the form. It's a kind of complex thing that every critic knows. You think the meaning is this, and so you look at the configuration of the object and you say, "Well, that can't be what the meaning of it is, because of this." So there's a process of rational equilibrium that takes place, until you more or less arrive at some idea as to what it's about and how it conveys that meaning. I thought that took care of a lot of cases, until it came to me one day that the Brillo box by Harvey satisfies that much—I didn't think, by the way, that that was the whole shebang. I mean, I didn't think that was the definition of art. But I thought those were pieces of it, and then I'd see what else I could come up with. But there was Harvey's box, and I thought, "Well it's got meaning. It's about Brillo." I knew that Warhol's wasn't about Brillo. And secondly, it embodies its meaning because it proclaims certain things about Brillo which Warhol's box certainly doesn't do.

And I thought, suddenly, that I'd made a fundamental mistake, the mistake being that, like anybody who was around in the 1960s, I'd read Clement Greenberg's famous article "Avant-Garde and Kitsch," and I was fairly snooty about commercial art. I think probably Andy would have said that I was snooty, because I would have said, "Well commercial art's not art." I think everybody in New York would have said something like that. And suddenly I realized, why not? Warhol would have said there's a difference between art and commercial art. He was very successful as a commercial artist, but he wanted to be an artist, as he said. Although being an artist turned out to mean just being a commercial artist, in a certain sense. Then I began to think that Warhol's gotten a lot of credit for the *Brillo Box* that really belongs to Jim Harvey. And I began to think about how I would address Harvey's box from the perspective of an art critic. I thought it was a brilliant piece of work. I'll just describe it very briefly, although as I say, it's probably as familiar to you as a picture of your mother on the dresser. It's got this red form and a white band between these two red banks—it's like a river of whiteness. And there is the word "Brillo"; the vowels are in red and the consonants in blue. So it's red, white and blue, and here's this river going through it. It becomes a kind of paean to patriotism: red, white and blue, and to cleanliness or sanitation, because it cleanses aluminum fast, cuts grease and so forth, with exclamation points. That river runs all the way around the Brillo box. So it tells you, it embodies its meaning: "Brillo will do it all for you. You'll be a patriot and you'll be clean. And how could you not use it, as against S.O.S.? Which sounds dangerous."

There's also some art history, because after all Jim Harvey was part of the art world. He was using hard-edge abstraction in this design. He was using Ellsworth Kelly or possibly Leon Polk Smith in composing the Brillo box. That was the gist of the kind of thing you'd want to say about Harvey. It's a little pathetic when you think about him. I don't know what else he did, but we found out that when he applied for a grant and they said, "What do you do?" he said, "I am a freelance package designer." There's a beautiful picture of Warhol giving Jim Harvey one of the *Brillo Boxes*. It was in *Newsweek* magazine, as a matter of fact. And then Jim Harvey died, and that's the last of him so far as the history of art is concerned, until now, when we're trying this resurrection. Thinking how immortal Warhol's *Brillo Box* is, there's a kind of derivative immortality that goes to Jim Harvey because it's his box.

But the really interesting question is, what is Warhol's *Brillo Box* about? What's the meaning of that? I knew it couldn't be about Brillo. It couldn't be about Brillo because there were about eight other kinds of cartons in the same show that it was in, at the Stable Gallery in 1964—at that momentous, at least for me momentous, exhibition. There was a Kellogg's corn flakes box, there was a Del Monte peach-half box, there was, I think, a Heinz ketchup box, et cetera, et cetera. And Warhol did them all, but the Brillo box is the only one you remember. Jim Harvey deserves all the credit. He was a far better designer, naturally, than anybody who did the Kellogg's box. Though each of the designs has got its rhetoric, you might say. You can tell just by looking at the signature of Kellogg's—it's like a doctor would write on a prescription. This proclaims that it's healthy if you eat it, as people did. I mean, they went to Battle Creek, Michigan, and just swilled down corn flakes and drank the water. But I thought whatever Warhol was interested in, it had to be all those things, not just Brillo. And moreover, what was the rhetoric? Warhol didn't have any. It was very uninflected. He was just presenting you with these things. I suddenly realized I didn't know the first thing about Warhol. Because I couldn't answer the question of what they were about, and I didn't know what they embodied. Because anything that his Brillo box embodied had equally to be embodied by any one of the cartons that he represented.

And then the whole question got complicated when Mike Bidlo also made some Brillo boxes. They had been made by a lot of people by this time—Richard Pettibone and Elaine Sturtevant. So it's out there and a lot of people mean different things by it. But whatever Mike meant by it certainly couldn't have been what Warhol meant by it, even though what Mike did was to appropriate the installation of *Brillo Boxes* that was at the Pasadena Art Museum in 1969. What does Mike mean? Whatever Mike Bidlo is after, as an artist, it's the same thing that a number of other people practicing appropriation are after. But it can't figure in what Warhol is doing. So I'm imagining a show of three Brillo boxes. They look indiscernible. But they are very distinct objects. Not simply in terms of when they were made and certainly not in terms of what they look like, because they all look exactly the same. But they have different meanings, they answer to different art historical imperatives and different critical imperatives. That's where I am, right at this point.

I'd like to carry the analysis out a little bit further. And I'm going to end by reporting the best thing that happened at the Brillo box conference in Nuremberg. Mike Bidlo came not with the original Brillo box, but one of his own Brillo boxes. It hardly fit into a taxi. Mike said, "Arthur, I'm not much of a talker, but I'd like to do a performance." I said, "Why not? I think people would be thrilled if you did a performance." After the talking was finished we went out and came back, and there were two tables. There was this great table, and Mike whisked, like a magician, the cloth. And it was his Brillo box, of course. And then behind it, he whisked a cloth off a bucket of soapy water and a pile of Brillo, which he'd gotten in Nuremberg, somehow. And he began to erase, scrub off, the Brillo box. It was very difficult. He'd never tried that before. It was plywood, after all, and it was painted with acrylic, and it dried very, very hard. Mike sweated. He's a big man and a strong man, but he said, "You people have got to help me." So all the art students came up, and there they were, working away. And they felt that they were at a moment of true art historical significance. Thank you.

2001

I'm Arthur Danto. I've been the art critic for *The Nation* magazine for about seventeen years, and for much longer than that I've been a professor of philosophy at Columbia University. A few years ago, here at Kamp Kippy, I talked a bit on the idea of beauty. It was a talk based on an essay for an exhibition at the Hirshhorn Museum called "Regarding Beauty" that I'd been invited to write by Olga Viso and Neal Benezra. And it was primarily in my capacity, I think, as a philosopher that they asked me to do that. They wanted some background in philosophical aesthetics, and I was certainly glad to do that.

I think that exhibition was a consequence of a rather well-known set of remarks by the critic Dave Hickey made in the early 1990s, at a panel, the title of which was "What's Happening Now." When Dave was asked what he thought the defining issue of the 1990s would be, he was daydreaming, and he blurted out, "Beauty . . . the defining issue of the 1990s will be beauty." That turned out to be a somewhat galvanizing remark, in the sense that people thought, "Yes, yes, there hasn't been much attention paid to beauty in the last while."

But it didn't pan out, I have to say. In the 1990s there were a number of conferences, a few panel discussions, some anthologies published, and some exhibitions, culminating in the Hirshhorn show, but so far as I could tell, no one actually producing art was making some tremendous turn from whatever they were doing to the production of beauty, in consequence of what Hickey said or in consequence of anything internal to their own agenda. I think in retrospect one has to recognize that, given the character of the art world, that was almost inevitable. The art world since the 1960s—since some rather intense conceptual investigation, some of it conducted by philosophers, but mostly by artists doing philosophy in a very practical way—has been an extraordinarily pluralistic place, so pluralistic that, structurally speaking, it's probably impossible that there would be a significant next thing. Almost as though the whole phase of history in which there would be structurally next things, like the move from traditional painting to modernism—nothing like that I think can take place.

I think the reason is almost obvious. Since artists like Beuys, artists like Warhol, artists like those who participated in the Fluxus movement, it's been tolerably clear that anything can be a work of art. Anything whatever. There's no longer any merit in the kind of question people used to ask, "Can this be art?

Can that be art?" The answer is just always going to be yes, it can be—constrained only by certain kinds of moral limits, if you will. If Valerie Solanas had actually killed Warhol and said, "That's my artwork," well, it might've been an artwork. It certainly could've been an artwork, but that doesn't justify her in having done it, nor would it be an excusing condition under the law. But given the elasticities and constant negotiation within moral life, anything pretty much can be done. I'm always astounded when I come here and see what people are doing. I never would've anticipated anything like it. But I certainly would never imagine somebody saying, "That's not art," in the way in which people said that quite freely in the 1950s and 1960s, of things that had no obvious way of being anything except art. For example, I remember Hilton Kramer saying of Judy Chicago's *Dinner Party*, "Well, it's just not art." Now we know that's over the hill. Anything can be art. But not everything can be beautiful. You know, therefore, that the concept of beauty is operating at a very different level from the concept of a work of art.

Hickey says in the preface of a book of essays called *The Invisible Dragon* [1993] that his statement about beauty, what he called a "goof," encountered an uncomprehending silence. And that silence, I think, he took as evidence that nobody had been for a very long time, in the art world at least, thinking about beauty as a serious artistic question. That may very well be because of the fact that the concept of beauty itself had undergone, over a very long time, a kind of trivialization. The received wisdom on the idea of beauty was that, well, beauty is in the eye of the beholder, a thought often attributed to the eighteenth-century thinker David Hume. And Hume indeed said beauty is in the mind of the beholder, but he thought everything was in the mind of the beholder. Hume belonged to the school of empiricist philosophers that flourished, in England particularly, in the eighteenth century. He says that, in addition to colors and feelings being in the mind, beauty, virtue and vice are in the mind. And since everything's in the mind, you can't distinguish between beauty and justice on the one hand and the perception of red or the feeling of pain on the other. But people never bothered to read what Hume actually said, and the idea was that you could dismiss beauty for that reason.

Hume believed, as a matter of fact, that there's probably as much uniformity in the judgment of beauty, or, for that matter, in moral judgments, as there is in sensation, that feelings and perceptions are probably pretty much the same throughout the human community. Of course, they didn't know a lot of anthropology in the eighteenth century; not until the end of the eighteenth century had Captain Cook begun to come back with strange reports from the South Seas. But I think Hume was probably right, and the reason people tended to think that there was so much diversity in the concept of beauty was because they were inclined to think that the production of art was connected with the production of beauty, and then they thought that what aborigines in different cultures were doing was trying to produce beautiful objects and failing abysmally, when as a matter of fact that wasn't the idea, obviously, at all. They were involved in far deeper things than the production of beauty.

Another bit of trivialization was the somewhat puritanical idea that beauty is only skin deep. But how deep should beauty be? Beauty really is on the skin, on the surface of things. Beautiful surfaces is what beauty is all about. Certainly the notion of beautification tended at least to render any preoccupation with beauty somewhat frivolous. If you look on Yahoo and type in "beauty," you're going to find a lot about cosmetics. You're not going to find anything philosophically very deep. I think it's because of that association that people have thought there's not much to beauty. And the philosophers certainly didn't help. In the 1930s, there was something called an emotivist theory of aesthetic language, according to which, to say something is beautiful is like emitting a long enthusiastic whistle in its presence—Wow!—and the thought was that "beautiful" didn't have any cognitive content.

But I don't think any of those considerations that are part of the trivialization of the concept can explain what seems to me to have been a characteristic of art in the twentieth century, namely a kind of hostility to beauty, a kind of feeling that was almost a hatred of beauty. There's a wonderful line in Rimbaud's poem *A Season in Hell*, where early on, Rimbaud, the writer, the narrator, at any rate, says, "One evening I sat Beauty on my knees, and I found her bitter, and I injured her." That was said in 1873, when Rimbaud wrote that extraordinary poem. The poet paid a terrible price for that dereliction, which I think is an important thing to remember as the poem unfurls. He goes truly through hell—it is a season in hell, and the precipitating event was the injury of beauty. But now I think people injure beauty in a regular kind of way. The question is why. That interests me a great deal, and lately my speculations on the topic have concerned themselves a bit with that. Where did that hostility come from?

Early in 2000 I shared a platform with Jean Clair, who's the director of the Picasso Museum in Paris. If you follow French aesthetic current events, you're aware that Jean Clair has become an exceedingly forceful spokesman against contemporary art. That's a fairly serious business in France, where so much of art is subsidized by the government, and government is always looking for ways to save money. Jean Clair has become something of a conservative hero for the articles he's written in *Figaro* and elsewhere. So *le contemporain* has a kind of political aura that contemporary art as an expression doesn't have in the United States.

Jean Clair and I had been invited, among others, to Tilburg University in the Brabant in the Netherlands, and Jean Clair offered an assessment of what he called "a new aesthetic," which had overtaken what he called "the aesthetics of taste," the eighteenth-century idea of taste. The new aesthetic, he said, was the aesthetics of disgust. The aesthetics of disgust is a kind of neat little thing you can say in French. You can say that from *goût*, which is the word for taste, we've gone to *dégoût*, which is the term for disgust. As a kind of curatorial tour de force, Jean Clair showed a great number of slides which he thought expressed this aesthetic, and he actually blames this transformation in aesthetic perception on Marcel Duchamp. It is interesting that he should do that, since he organized the inaugural exhibition at the Centre Pompidou, which was on Duchamp.

Whatever the case, he and I had a discussion. But I got very interested in the notion of disgust, actually, for a number of reasons. The philosopher Kant talks a great deal—well, not a great deal, but he does talk about disgust. In fact, I don't know any philosopher other than Kant who talked about disgust. In 1763, he wrote *Observations on the Feeling of Beauty and the Sublime*, and in that book he talks about disgust as the antinomy of beauty, not ugliness. The reasoning Kant has for that is anything ugly can be given a beautiful representation, and he thought there are a great many cases of things that are actually ugly that are very beautiful when they're represented by artists.

But he thought the one thing you couldn't do that to was disgust, the disgusting. He felt that the disgusting could in no way be beautified.

I began to correspond with a psychologist who's been doing some empirical work on disgust, a man named Jonathan Haidt at the University of Virginia. And he is more or less trying to identify what he calls core disgust. Core disgust, the things that everybody would typically find disgusting. Darwin mentions disgust in his book *The Expression of the Emotions in Man and Animals*. There is a facial expression for it, there are wonderful drawings in Darwin's book which show anger, et cetera. If I say, "Show disgust," anybody can do it. There is a disgust reflex. It's usually, typically, elicited by food. But it varies—even Darwin, because he traveled, recognized that it's not the same from culture to culture. He concludes, or at least anthropologists have concluded, that there is a core set of "disgust elicitors," that more or less everybody in a given culture would agree on. There's a whole cultural feeling that you don't eat certain things. But Haidt says people who were brought up with animals—feral children—never show disgust. They still don't eat poisonous things, but that's not the kind of thing that disgust is supposed to deal with. So it's somewhat curious. I wrote him and I said, is there such a thing as core beauty, things that everybody would find beautiful? He's never done that work, but I'm under the impression that there would be. It would be the kind of thing maybe that would show up in John Coltrane, a song like *My Favorite Things*, you know, blue sky, and so forth. I think that, despite what Darwin and John Haidt said, there's a lot of cultural invariance there. I read an account of somebody keeping people prisoner in Central America, and he said, "This is how we break people's will. You put them in a cell, a dark place, with a lot of vermin, and give them lousy food, et cetera, et cetera, and before long their will is broken." Human beings are pretty much the same, I think, everywhere, and it'd be interesting if there would be a kind of core concept of beauty.

So what accounts for the hostility, the need to injure beauty? When I was writing a book on Robert Mapplethorpe, I asked a photographer who was playing with pinhole cameras what he thought of Mapplethorpe. He said, "He's a *pompier*," a French expression for somebody too preoccupied with elegance, a kind of term they used for "academic." He was not at all disgusted by the sadomasochist depictions in Mapplethorpe, but he hated the beauty. I'm really keen to try to discover the answer to that, because my thought is that there's something deeply important about the concept of beauty, and I'd like to see it somehow or other redeemed. I'd like to execute what one might call a philosophical redemption of the idea of beauty. Not that there's any way of internally connecting it with art, but it ought to be a permissible option for artists to create beauty. Somehow or other the hatred of beauty has got to be overcome. I've been trying to figure out how that's to be done. I don't think you can do it by conceptual analysis. In the late nineteenth century, people began to think that beauty would be able to do all that religion traditionally had done—that beauty, and hence art, would answer most of the moral needs of human beings. You find that kind of statement over and over again. It comes up in Edwardian times, hence I speak of it as Edwardian aesthetics. It comes up particularly in the writing of a philosopher I greatly admire named G. E. Moore—not much read anymore, but when I was a graduate student, widely read, but not for the reasons that he was read by the people who worshipped him, the Bloomsbury Group, like Virginia Woolf and Roger Fry and Clive Bell and E. M. Forster. They thought he was a great, great thinker, and it was because Moore thought that the perception of beauty and human friendship were the great moral things, the great paradigms of moral life. And the Bloomsbury people tried to embody those virtues in their life. But this exaltation of beauty produced a backlash.

The long and short of this thought is that the Dadaists felt that they were doing something of deep significance by producing works of art which were the antithesis of beauty. As Max Ernst said, they tried to make people scream when they saw them. That's because they blamed the people who made the First World War for doing something unthinkable, and they thought if they could just rob them of beauty . . . well, beauty had to be very significant if artists could think by robbing people of beauty they could make a significant political statement.

It would be interesting to archaeologize what the attitude toward beauty would have been, up to World War I, and realize the moral energy that went into Dada, in those artists thinking that they could eliminate beauty from art. I think it was a conceptual discovery that you could make art without beauty.

Nobody up to that point had seriously thought about that, before Dada, and I don't think any philosopher would've been able to come up with those ideas. But Dada did, and I think that's a prevailing view. I think the idea of anti-beauty is connected with political criticism and that it has lingered on, and that conceivably, if one managed to archaeologize the notion and explain how this happened step by step, some of the animus would be leached out of the concept of beauty. In other words, I think that for artists today, it's much more reasonable for them to produce something that's disgusting, like Paul McCarthy, for example, so that in a way, there is something to Jean Clair's views. But I don't think that's the whole story, and I don't think the explanation with Duchamp solves it.

I'd say just this, in conclusion. Last summer when I was here, I worked out my response to Jean Clair, and it's published on the Internet, in a journal of Duchamp studies published by Rhonda Shearer. It's called *Tout-Fait*, which is her idea of what the French equivalent of "readymade" would be. I dedicated that essay to Kippy, because I wrote it here, and I was reminded when I was writing it of Rilke writing the *Duino Elegies* in Duino Castle in Trieste. He'd been invited by the Princess of Thurn und Taxis to do a period of residence. I thought of Rilke's great, great line that beauty is only the beginning of terror, talking about the angelic order. And I thought, well, certainly I'm no poet, and least of all would I, if a poet, be comparable to Rilke. But I think Kippy really is the Princess of Thurn und Taxis. [*laughter*]

At any rate, angels are interesting. Jacob wrestled with an angel all night long. Wrestling with beauty is not like that. Bill Berkson sent me an email. He said something like beauty is such a mangled, saddened idea. "Maybe," he said, "you can straighten it out." I prized that line—a mangled, saddened idea. He said the reality is not, but the idea is. Wrestling with beauty is a bit like wrestling with a walrus. That is to say, you can get a grip on an angel, I'm pretty sure, but a walrus is a very different kind of creature to wrestle with. At any rate, I'm spending my week up here wrestling with a walrus. [*laughter*] Thank you.

2002

I'm Arthur Danto, and most people who are mainly in the art world would know my critical pieces in *The Nation* magazine, but in truth, I've spent most of my mature life in the philosophy department at Columbia University. People have been asking me, "What are you writing now?" and the answer is I'm writing a book on beauty, which I hope to have finished, at least in a fairly good but rough draft, by the time I leave here. It's been a wonderful place to write.

Beauty is not what one thinks of as a cutting-edge subject, and I have to admit that it was never a burning issue for me either; at least as a philosopher, I had no interest, really, in aesthetics. As a graduate student, I had to study aesthetics and read a certain distance into the canonical literature. But I had mostly artist friends when I moved to New York, and I could never see that what the philosophers were saying had to do with what the artists were doing, nor could I see that it had very much relationship to the kinds of discussions one would have with artists. I did have the good luck to take a course in aesthetics with Susanne K. Langer, whom I've greatly admired as a thinker, and with whom I formed actually a warm personal relationship. But much as I liked her, I could never apply anything that she taught to what was happening in the fairly exciting art world of New York at that time, in the late 1950s.

I gave one of my early papers on the philosophy of art—I always think that there is some connection between what's happening in philosophy and what's happening in art—at the University of Pittsburgh, and a man named Nicholas Rescher, who's written about a hundred books, said proudly, "I've never written one line in aesthetics," and that was meant to be refutation of my essay. But the great philosopher of science, Peter Hempel, whom I adored, came up to me and he said, "Arthur, you know, it really reminds me of conversations I had with the people in Dada in Berlin." I so enjoy the old installation photographs from the first Dada exhibition in 1922 in Berlin, and it gives me great pleasure to think that Peter Hempel was there talking with Hannah Höch and John Heartfield and George Grosz and all those extraordinary people. If you look at those photographs, there's a poster that says "Die Kunst ist tot"—art is dead— "Es lebe die neue Maschinenkunst Tatlins"—long live the new machine art of Tatlin. I can just hear Hempel saying, "Yeah, yeah, we believe the same thing about metaphysics. Metaphysics is dead, long live the logical philosophy of Frege."

The idea of the death of metaphysics—probably the impulse comes from Wittgenstein, whose book, the *Tractatus Logico-Philosophicus*, was published I think around the same time as the Dada exhibition in Berlin. In that book, Wittgenstein says the propositions that philosophers have made are neither true nor false, but nonsense. There's no way in which you can answer the question, but simply show the senselessness, and you do that through the logical clarification of language. What they didn't understand was the logic of their language, and what you get in the *Tractatus* is an effort at a kind of canonical notation in which you can't express nonsense. It would be somewhat interesting as artists to read a little bit into the *Tractatus*, because he did have a pictorial theory of meaning. He thought of certain basic sentences as pictures of facts and so forth, and I don't think he had yet the idea that there could be nonsensical pictures. But he was, though very radical as a philosopher, quite conservative, I guess, aesthetically. He came from the Vienna of Klimt and Kokoschka.

I had never been able to get any traction in the galleries, or in studios, with aesthetics, or see any philosophical connection between philosophy and art at all, until the 1960s, when I encountered Pop art, and particularly the exhibition of Warhol's, the *Brillo Boxes* and other cartons, at the Stable Gallery. That seemed to me finally to open up the possibility of a genuine philosophical way of thinking about art, because Warhol had produced these simulacra of Brillo boxes. The deep question for me was, how do you ground the difference between them and real Brillo boxes, one being a work of art and the other one not. You realized that you couldn't answer the question visually, or at least not in an interesting way visually. The differences couldn't be visual. I realized that a philosophy of art had to disregard the visual in that way. The moment you can begin to think of things that way, you suddenly have the form of a basic philosophical question.

I've worked with the *Brillo Boxes* for a very, very, very long time. They were my inspiration. Although, thinking back on it, I talked about the Brillo boxes rather than the Kellogg's corn flakes box or the Del Monte peach halves box or the Heinz ketchup box, or the other boxes—it has to have been because the Brillo box was more beautiful in some way. It was designed by an Abstract Expressionist painter, who made his livelihood as what he described as a freelance package designer. His name was James Harvey. And I've been on the trail of James Harvey. He died very young. There is a photograph of Warhol giving him one of his *Brillo Boxes*. We found recently a photograph of James Harvey kneeling in front of one of his own large Abstract Expressionist paintings, holding the Brillo box, and it was very moving to see it. He was successful, or beginning to be successful. He had a wonderful review in the *New York Times* by Brian O'Doherty, and sold out his show at the Graham Gallery, but he didn't live long enough to benefit as an artist. A colleague of mine in Germany and I hope one day to organize a James Harvey memorial show, with the Brillo box, and with as many of his paintings as we can find.

My reason for not thinking about aesthetics, in any case, was probably because of Duchamp, and because Duchamp really wasn't prepared to give aesthetics the time of day. I was really moved by the way in which Duchamp described his readymades—at a much later date. He did the readymades around 1913, 1917. It was not that easy, evidently, to identify something as a readymade, because it had to have no aesthetic merit whatsoever. That was Duchamp's criterion. It should be absolutely anaesthetic, Duchamp said, undistinguished. It interested me that something could be a work of art without aesthetics, and if it could be a work of art without aesthetic properties, then it seemed to me that aesthetic properties really didn't belong to the definition of art. It was the definition of art that I was deeply involved with—what are the necessary and sufficient conditions for something to be a work of art—and so you could write off questions of beauty right off the bat, since something could be a work of art without any aesthetic attributes at all.

That was the way things stood in the 1960s. I wrote my first paper in the philosophy of art—it was mostly about things that I'd seen at the Stable Gallery and the Green Gallery, and the few places that were showing Pop art. And Minimalism also; Bob Morris's big plywood cartons meant a lot to me, because, again, they seemed to me to have zero degree of aesthetic interest. The paper—it was called "The Artworld"—was published in the *Journal of Philosophy* in 1964. I've subsequently realized that there were a lot of people all over New York who were basically thinking about *minimalia*, you might say, the minimum kind of thing that can be an artwork. The Fluxus artists, whom

I didn't know about until the 1980s, for example. I explain that historically, through the impact of a number of Dr. Daisetsu Teitaro Suzuki's ideas, who was a colleague, in a way, at Columbia. He taught on the same floor where my office was. On the days that Dr. Suzuki would teach, the art world would come up to Columbia, and it was really fascinating to see who you'd see when the elevator door opened and people would walk out, asking, "Where is Dr. Suzuki's course?"

But the interest in aesthetics began for me in 1993, actually. I was already an art critic for *The Nation*, and leave it to *The Nation* to hire an art critic who thinks the definition of art has got nothing to do with visuality. But philosophy's philosophy and art's art. And 1993 was something of an extraordinary year, I think, as I go back and review what was happening at that time. Dave Hickey, for one thing, published a widely discussed—I don't know whether it was influential, but a widely discussed book, *The Invisible Dragon*, in which he talked about beauty becoming the defining problem of the 1990s. As a prediction I think it didn't get very far. And in 1993, you would've found very little empirical corroboration in the art world. For example, the 1993 Whitney Biennial was the famous biennial in which virtually the entire exhibition was made up of confrontationally political work of one sort or another. There may have been something beautiful there, but for the most part, the artists were interested in righting various injustices. Most of those ideas that surfaced in the 1993 Biennial were developed in the 1980s, I think, and it was almost the climax of that movement. The Whitney's director at that point, David Ross, had brought in Elisabeth Sussman, who was given sole responsibility for that show, and she selected this fairly incendiary show, which was widely resented, it seems to me, rightly or wrongly resented.

I was asked to speak at a conference in the early 1990s on the topic of beauty, despite the fact that I'd not ever really written on beauty or thought very deeply about it. I decided to give a talk about Robert Motherwell's "Elegies to the Spanish Republic." I did have a slide on that occasion; I had actually more than one slide. The slide was *Elegy to the Spanish Republic No. 172 (With Blood)*, which was painted in 1990. Of the powerful experiences that I've had of an aesthetic nature, one of them was seeing, quite unexpectedly, one of the Spanish Elegies in an exhibition of abstract art at the Museum of Modern Art, probably in the 1950s or '60s. I didn't know who did it, but it was an extraordinarily exciting painting, and I rushed over to see who had done it, and noticed the title. I went away thinking about it, but I wasn't an art critic at that point. I didn't try to think—I didn't think very deeply—it's the nature of most such experiences, that you have them and you think a bit about them, but you don't try to think very much about what explains them. Later, Motherwell had an exhibition at the Guggenheim Museum [1985], and in one of the early pieces that I wrote for *The Nation*, I talked about my experience with the Spanish Elegy—without knowing anything about it or really about the artist, I was literally stopped in my tracks by that painting. And inevitably, that went over fairly well with the artist. We saw a TV program, maybe it was *The News Hour*, I don't know, but Motherwell was being interviewed in his studio, and he was asked what he thought about critics, and Motherwell said, "I really don't read the critics" and so forth and so on. He said, "But, you know, somebody just wrote about this show," and he said, "And that is the person I paint for." And so, inevitably, we became friends. We began to correspond, and I would drive up to Greenwich, where he lived with Renate Ponsold, and I'd say we had a kind of brotherly relationship. There was a point where my younger daughter Ginger started dating his studio assistant, Mel Paskell, and Bob thought that we were going to be in-laws, and that that would be beautiful, and the wedding would take place out there.

Bob died in 1991, and his death was on my mind, and so the invitation to do this talk was a chance to think about the Spanish Elegies. I chose them because I thought they were beautiful, and because I thought in some sense they were political. After all, the title The Spanish Republic was not an accident. Bob did have a certain, as he said, international political side to him. I started to think about elegies, and elegies are discourses, beautiful words, as a general rule, that are uttered about the departed, about the dead. I began to wonder why beauty itself turns out to be appropriate at funerals, for example. I was very interested at that time in funerals. A lot of my students were gay, and a lot of them were dropping off with AIDS, and some of them began to design their own funerals, and beauty played a great role. I became interested in the question of why that should be the case—what is the psychological connection between reconciliation to death and beauty. I tried to write a bit of an analysis of that. I don't think we really know enough psychology. We've been I think shortchanged by academic psychology. We're not given the information, it seems to me, that we need for that kind of knowledge. But I thought that the beauty tends to put the death at a certain distance, that it's almost like seeing something in a philosophical way. In the course of thinking about Motherwell's paintings, I had the idea that what was interesting about the beauty of the painting was that it was internal to the meaning of the work, that its beauty connected with what it was about—not that there's anything beautiful about what it represented, namely the death of the second Spanish Republic. If you look at the forms, the forms look like shawled women standing next to charred and shattered posts, and so there are these oval forms and then those architectural forms, and sometimes you get two or three ovals against a very pale light, the kind of light that you'd see, for example, in the dawn in Piero's *Resurrection*, a very cold light. It would be wrong, obviously—not even morally permissible—to say how beautiful those shawled women next to the ruins of their houses look, but I thought that is in some way what they were about.

I went on, in the course of that talk, to give other examples of what I thought were cases of internal beauty, as I'd decided to call it, and to distinguish it from external beauty, where something's externally beautiful when it's not part of the meaning of it—for example, you can't connect it with the content of what it's about. The idea of internal beauty began to be something I could think about, and it was a piece of structure, if you see what I mean, and I thought you could do something with it. I began, for example, to think of it in connection with the Vietnam Veterans Memorial, which by common consent is a very beautiful work, and where it seemed to me that the beauty of it is internal to the meaning of it, that you see yourself reflected among the names of the dead in this highly polished stone. You walk down—it's almost an underground experience—and you encounter yourself reflected in that way. I thought a lot about the connection between those reflections and the names, the way you think about the *Water Lilies* of Monet, where the clouds are in the water and you really can't distinguish easily between water and sky. And I thought that its great success was due to that.

The man who raised the money for the Vietnam Veterans Memorial, a rifleman named Jan Scruggs, wrote a book about his experience, which is called *To Heal a Nation*. He felt that the country needed a monument, a memorial, and there was this big competition, there were 1,400 entries, and Maya Lin won. At first Jan Scruggs was shocked when he saw what had won—what was it, what is this thing, and so forth. He thought, well, is it a boomerang, is it a bat, what are we giving the people? But he said somebody told him, "You know, people are more sophisticated than you think," and that turned out really to be the case. People were deeply moved by it, and I thought they were being moved by it because of its elegiac quality, that the beauty played a role. I think to the degree that it's possible for a work of art to heal a nation, that would be the prime example I, at any rate, would be able to think of, and beauty played a major role there.

There are other examples. I mean, one can think of a great many examples, once one begins to think that way. There's a passage in Proust's *Remembrance of Things Past* which I've always found profoundly moving. It takes place in a little section of the book where the narrator, Marcel, goes back to a seaside hotel at Balbec—Cabourg—and his grandmother had died earlier, and one is really shocked to see how cold Marcel was, because she had loved him in a very overt and demonstrative way. The passage in the novel is very clinical and detached, and you said, well, he's a much colder person than I ever really could've believed, almost heartless. He goes back to Balbec, and he puts his grandmother's photograph on the table, and then he begins to weep. He begins to weep, and he is tortured by how cold he'd been, how he hadn't remembered the goodness of his grandmother when they were at Balbec, he was too busy chasing girls, and he didn't think about her, but he had since learned certain things, and he just can't basically enjoy his life at all. He's haunted by that death and by his own coldness. One day he goes for a walk after the rain, along a road where he and his grandmother used to be taken in the carriage of Madame de Villeparisis, and he passes by a stand of apple trees in bloom, and he begins to talk about these apple trees. He uses a lot of metaphorical language and a number of analogies between the apple trees and pink satin, apple trees and Japanese prints, and so forth. It must've been a stunning sight.

It's probably a sight that would take your breath away if you were to have seen it yourself. But in his case, his heart began to ease at that point. The experience of beauty seemed in some way to have begun the healing process.

I was invited to give the Carus Lectures for the American Philosophical Association this past Christmas, and it's a singular honor to be asked. There are three lectures delivered on successive days at the annual meeting. I decided I'd like to develop this—probably nobody's talked to the American Philosophical Association about beauty since its inception. It was a hundred years old on this occasion. But beauty is a traditional subject. It's a subject that Hegel and Kant and Hume devoted a great deal of thought to, and "The Critique of Aesthetic Judgment," Part I of the *Critique of Judgment,* is certainly the keystone of Kant's critical system. I thought, it'll be okay for these guys to hear something about beauty. I didn't know what I was getting into, to tell you the truth, but there are no question periods. It's as bad as the National Gallery—when I gave the Mellon Lectures, they wouldn't allow questions to be asked. You have to do each lecture in an hour at plenary session and so forth, but people were pretty interested, as it turned out. I called the lectures "The Abuse of Beauty," and I tried actually to give some kind of an answer to the question of whatever happened to beauty, and the lectures I was fairly pleased with. But it's one of the expectations that you'll publish these lectures as a book—well, three lectures doesn't actually make a book, I'm afraid. That's too thin a manuscript. In fact, most of the Carus Lectures that I'd ever read—they began in 1927; the first one was *Experience and Nature* by John Dewey—they're fairly thick books. I'm sure there's a certain amount of padding in all those books, but I knew that I had to make it larger. It was hard for me to do it, because I really wanted the lectures to have a kind of symmetry, embody a kind of form—have some internal beauty, if you like, as well as address the subject. It was hard to crack it, but once I came up here it turned out to be not that difficult to crack it. So that's what I'm writing on at this moment.

I have to say this before I end this. I felt fairly sheepish at the beginning writing about beauty, for the reasons that, as I say, in the tradition that I came up in as a philosopher, nobody could take aesthetics very seriously. Certainly my own philosophical reputation was based on fairly austere analyses that were addressed mainly to the profession. But as I worked, finally, on the lectures, I did get the sense that I was writing on maybe the most important thing I could've written on. I don't know yet why that was, but I was very, very taken with the way in which people responded in New York to the World Trade Center disaster. Immediately, everywhere, these little shrines appeared. A very vernacular kind of beauty, but they all had candles, they all had flowers—they all had balloons, or many of them had balloons. They had photographs and so forth of somebody who at least was beautiful in their eyes. And so I thought that the disposition to produce those kinds of objects in the face of that kind of sadness must be something very deeply connected with what it means to be human. I can't pretend that I'll be able to wind up with a good, clear understanding of that, but at any rate, that's what the book's about. Thanks.

2003

I'm Arthur Danto, and I have two credentials. I'm a professor of philosophy, have been most of my life at Columbia University, and then art critic for *The Nation*. Most people know me primarily as an art critic, but my main calling is as a philosopher. And people who read *The Nation* columns don't realize it, but they've been getting free lessons in philosophy for as long as those things have been printed, because I don't write about anything unless I can write about it in a philosophical way.

There are no slides tonight. I want to talk about this book of mine, which just came out. We got copies a couple of weeks ago, just in time to bring one up here, and I feel as though at the very least I owe a copy to A.S.A.P., because I've worked on various stages of the book over the years we've been coming here. Kippy says there are no photographs in my books, and generally that's true, and there are almost never any in the columns that I write for the magazine, because space is precious and pictures take up a lot of it. But in this case there actually are some photographs, because the book is based on three lectures I gave for the American Philosophical Association at its annual meeting in December of 2001. The reason there are pictures in it is because philosophers don't know anything about art as a general rule, but it would be silly for me to show those pictures to an audience like this, where everybody knows all the pictures that I would be showing. And I'm not going to talk about those pictures, at any rate.

I want to talk, first of all, about the title of the book. The title of the book is *The Abuse of Beauty*—and then it's got a subtitle, which isn't that important. People like the title, are intrigued by the title, and I thought I should at least begin by explaining the title, which comes from a poem by Arthur Rimbaud, written in 1873. It's called *A Season in Hell*. In the third line of the poem, Rimbaud writes: "One evening I sat Beauty on my knees, and I found her bitter and I abused her." The French is: "Un soir, j'ai assis la Beauté sur mes genoux.—Et je l'ai trouvée amère.—Et je l'ai injuriée." But I thought "injured her" would be a bad translation, because you can injure somebody unintentionally, but it's really clear that Rimbaud intentionally abused Beauty. In the first line of the poem, he writes: "Formerly, if I remember correctly, my life was a banquet where every heart was open and all the

to find works of art that were really not to be told apart from ordinary objects that weren't works of art. My initiating example was the Brillo box exhibition at the Stable Gallery on East 74th Street at that time. That, and a show of Robert Morris's big wooden structures at the Green Gallery on 57th Street. I was very excited by both bodies of work because for the first time, at least in my experience as a philosopher, art became philosophically interesting. It was interesting before that time, but it wasn't philosophically interesting for me, or at least I didn't know any way of making it philosophically interesting. But then it began to be, because you had objects which were artworks which were just indiscernible from ordinary objects.

I began to think that giving a definition of art was going to suddenly become an interesting question. How do you do it, when you want to include in a definition everything that's a work of art but exclude everything that's not, where the things outside the class of works of art and the things inside the class of works of art look pretty much the same? That question got to be urgent in the 1960s.

The kind of philosophy that I did—or do, I think, still—is called analytical philosophy. It's conceptual analysis, and since everybody here will have taken at least an elementary course in philosophy, they will know what I am talking about. That kind of philosophy essentially consists of attempting to arrive at a definition which gives you an analysis of a concept. It really begins with the Socratic dialogues of Plato. Socrates takes some term in use—"justice," "knowledge," "love"—and asks, "Well, what do you mean by that?" Somebody offers some characterization of the meaning, and then Socrates finds a counterexample, and then the speaker tries to adjust his definition to accommodate the counterexample. Then the dialogue peters out, and it ends, one way or another.

The definition of art had not been particularly urgent down the centuries, because art history was essentially a fairly stable thing. People were producing what Plato, or Aristotle, at the very least, said artworks are, namely imitations of something. And that more or less held. Beauty wasn't much of a problem, because there was a sort of standard view of what beauty was as what pleases the eye. The formulation in Saint Thomas, for example, captures the Aristotelian idea, and nobody thought that there was an extra question about beauty.

There was a polemic in the late 1950s, particularly due to a well-known philosopher, Ludwig Wittgenstein, that the whole program of looking for definitions was, as a matter of fact, pointless. You don't need a definition of anything. Why look around for a definition? He gave a famous example in a book called *Philosophical Investigations*, namely games. He asked, what would be the single defining property of games? And he began listing all the different kinds of games he could think of: hopscotch, ring around the rosie, chess, Monopoly, and so forth. He said, don't say that there is some common attribute; tell me what it is. Look for it; look and see. And do you really appeal to that common attribute where you say this is a game, that's a game, and so forth and so on? He said, finally, no, there is no common attribute. It wouldn't make us any wiser. We don't need these definitions, and there's no end to the number of games. This was fairly revolutionary to have said, because it meant that almost the entire agenda of philosophy for two thousand years was misdirected. A number of Wittgenstein's disciples attempted to apply that to the concept of art. The general idea was that it's impossible to give a definition of art because works of art of novel kinds keep coming along. And it's unnecessary. We all know what the works of art really are. One writer—I've used the example before—said, imagine a warehouse full of heterogeneous objects, chairs and tables and so forth, and ask somebody to go in and pick out the works of art, and people will do it. They might not know how to classify photographs, they might not know how to deal with certain things, but mostly they'll know which the works of art are. It'd be the kind of things they'd seen in museums.

Suddenly, it seemed to me that, well, neither Wittgenstein nor his followers ever considered the possibility of distinguishing artworks from games. What about that? With Fluxus, suddenly games began to be works of art. If you go to the Silverman Collection in Detroit, you'll see cases full of these dumb little games, games in which you have to get little pellets into holes in the face of a clown and so forth, the kinds of games everybody's familiar with. These are works of art. Fluxus was extremely fertile in turning out things like that. A man named George Brecht, whose work the founder of Fluxus, George Maciunas, admired a great deal, was turning a light switch on and then turning a light switch off. That's one of his works, a performance. Could be a piece of music, could be a composition, even. It was very difficult to classify it as far as a classical genre of art was concerned, but it was a work of art. Maciunas liked it because it was one that you couldn't tell from an ordinary thing. At that point, people in Fluxus and elsewhere in the art world were interested in overcoming the gap, as they would put it, between art and life, to try to make works of art that look so much like ordinary things that you couldn't tell the difference between them.

Everybody here is familiar with what was driving that. It was John Cage's ideas about noise and music and certain ideas coming out of Zen from Dr. Suzuki's seminar. Dr. Suzuki used to teach on my floor in Philosophy Hall at Columbia, and for a time I used to listen to his lectures, such as they were, and I thought a great deal about those questions too. What was art and what was not art? That seemed to me an urgent question when you couldn't tell the difference. With the warehouse example, you should be able to pick out examples: "This is a work of art, this isn't, this is a work of art." But suddenly when you've got pairs of similar things, one of which is a work of art and the other one not, it wasn't that easy to pick them out. They were identical twins as far as that was concerned, but one falls in the class of art and the other one not.

So it was around that time that I began to get really interested in the definition of art, and I was struck by—well, I don't know what I was struck by at that time, but I've since been struck by the following consideration, that the idea of beauty, which would've been uppermost in people's minds if they were undertaking to give a definition of art earlier, had simply fallen out of the picture. Nobody talked about beauty. The works of art didn't seem to be deeply preoccupied with beauty. You can say that Warhol's *Brillo Box* is more beautiful than the five other boxes that he showed at the Stable Gallery, but he didn't get any credit for that. I always love to bring in the name of James Harvey, who designed the Brillo box. It was the best piece of commercial art, but it doesn't redound to Warhol's credit at all.

Beauty had fallen out of the picture in art, and it seemed to have fallen out of the picture in philosophy. When people in philosophy in the 1960s were undertaking to give definitions—I feel deeply that there are certain pulses in the history of culture—the same thing that happened in art was in some way happening in philosophy at the same time. Don't ask me why or to offer an explanation of that. But it was interesting to me that people in philosophy who undertook to give some sort of an analytical definition of art—there wasn't an epidemic, there were three or four people—never mentioned beauty. Richard Wollheim, who coined the term Minimalism, was interested in the question of what the minimal properties are that something has to have in order to be a work of art. He talked about monochrome painting, and he talked about readymades, and so forth. He was interested in how you pick out instances of art. I thought that really there was no longer a possibility, even, to pick out the works of art. But he didn't mention beauty. George Dickie, who offered a definition, didn't really mention beauty. Neither did I, I have to say, in the effort I made at a fairly primitive piece of defining.

What interested me was just this historical question—I think of myself sometimes as doing what I call philosophical art history—namely, when do the concepts change, not when did this period end and that period begin, although that's kind of interesting, too. But when do the concepts undergo change? I was interested in such facts as these: that the enabling papers for the John Simon Guggenheim Foundation, when it was set up in 1925, stated the intention to subsidize two groups of people, those who advanced knowledge and those who created beauty. That's the way in which, if you were an artist, you were going to be given a Guggenheim Fellowship. It would be really interesting for an art historian to see who were the people who got Guggenheims in the first five or six years—were they actually creating beauty? By 1930, if you look at the logo for the Institute for Advanced Studies at Princeton, it's a logo which has got two women on it, one naked, that's knowledge, and one with some clothes on, that's beauty. And knowledge and beauty, truth and beauty, those were the two things to which the Institute for Advanced Studies was originally dedicated. But by 1965, in this period in which I think the revolution in art, and to some degree the revolution in philosophy, or at least the philosophy of art, took place, beauty dropped totally out of the question. I think it's because of Sputnik, by and large. I think the reason the National Endowment for the Arts was founded was because of this: "Artists have got crazy ideas, who knows when we might be able to use something in the Cold War." There's no beauty at all, but crazy ideas—look at Leonardo, I mean he designed fortifications and so forth. I think that's what they hoped to get for national defense from the National Endowment. There were a few conservative senators who thought beauty was part of the picture, but it wasn't.

So I got interested in that question, whatever happened to beauty, why did it drop out of everybody's sensibility, why did it drop out of art, and so forth. In a way, that's what this book tries to give an answer to—why did it disappear, and what does it mean that it did disappear, and where does it stand today?

I will just say one thing to close this off, because my main hope is that everybody will read the book. But this was really interesting. I learned this from Olga Viso, a curator at the Hirshhorn. In 1999, she and Neal Benezra put on an exhibition called "Regarding Beauty," and I was invited to write an essay for that book. And I tried to talk a little bit about why there was somehow or other an interest in beauty in the 1990s. There's probably a simple answer to it, but there's probably a deep answer as well. The simple answer is that Dave Hickey began to write about it. The complex answer would be why did Dave write about it, and nobody knows that. Olga said that three years earlier she and Neal had put on a show called "Distemper," which was about the idea of dissonance in contemporary art. And people told Olga, "You know what's interesting about these objects? Some of them are really pretty beautiful." That's what inspired Olga to do the "Regarding Beauty" show. So you start thinking, was there some turn in art history where suddenly, from dissonance, distemper, you're interested in beauty? I thought maybe if I could nail that down, that would be kind of fascinating. I didn't do it at the time, but I've thought about it a lot since. I thought, suppose you decide you want to do two shows, "Distemper" and "Regarding Beauty." Since most of the dissonant objects are beautiful, or people find them beautiful, why do two shows? Why not just have two entrances or two banners, and just use the same objects? So a couple comes to the museum and she says, "Oh, I'd love to see 'Regarding Beauty,'" and he says, "I kind of like the idea of 'Distemper.' I'll meet you in an hour." They go in through these two entrances, and then, of course, inevitably, they meet one another, and she says, "You're in the wrong show," and he says, "No, *you're* in the wrong show." How do you resolve that?

The book is a little bit about that kind of a question—how do you resolve that you're in the wrong show?

Here's at least a clue. If you were going to do a show of dissonant objects, I think everybody would agree that Duchamp's urinal is a dissonant object. I mean, now not so much, but it would've been dissonant to put a urinal in an art gallery. It certainly was at the beginning. So you put that in. We do know that Duchamp's patron, Walter Arensberg, said that what "R. Mutt" was doing was drawing attention to a lovely form. So I'll assume that he thought it was beautiful and what Marcel had done had been to draw our attention to the aesthetics of everyday plumbing.

I think the urinal is beautiful. But is the work beautiful? Is it intrinsic to the work that it should be beautiful? I start working with that question of whether the beauty of the urinal is part of the meaning of the work. Then all we have to do is to find out what's the meaning of *Fountain*, and we can decide whether the beauty is internal or external, intrinsic or extrinsic. That's what the docents should be able to do. They say, "No, this is not intrinsic to the work. This beauty is not intrinsic to the work. It's extrinsic to the work. It's intrinsic to the urinal, but it's not intrinsic to the work." That distinction between what I call internal and external beauty is I suppose the central philosophical, and maybe the central cultural contribution of the book, and I make a great deal of it. You've got to interpret the work to find out whether, as a matter of fact, the beauty is really part of the work or simply part of the object. To get to the bottom of that, you've got to read chapter five. Thanks very much.

2004

I'm Arthur Danto. Most people in the art world are likely to know me from pieces that I write for *The Nation* magazine, where I've been the art critic for the past twenty years—actually, it will be twenty years in October. But my day job, as they say in the art world, is to be a philosopher, which is an odd way to make a living, but that's how I have, and it was just a fluke, really, that I found myself an art critic. Nobody can prepare for a career like that, and philosophy is probably as good a preparation as any. In truth, it was a piece of philosophical writing that landed me that job. I published a book in 1981 called *The Transfiguration of the Commonplace*, which was a philosophy of art based on problems that I encountered in the art world in the 1960s, works that had what struck me as extremely interesting philosophical properties, but I didn't write about them quite at that time.

The transfiguration of the commonplace—well, the idea of transfiguration has somewhat religious connotations, obviously. The Transfiguration is in Saint Matthew, where the problem is almost like the problem of 1960s art, in the sense that you're dealing with a god who is also a human being, which hadn't strictly happened in the history of things before. Most gods, I expect, really looked like gods, but Jesus didn't look like a god, he just looked like the man next door. And the question was, how do you validate the claim that you are not merely the Son of God, but God? That was very like the kinds of problems, it seemed to me, that the art world was beginning to present in the 1960s, when you would have a work of art which looked exactly like an object with which you were very familiar which wasn't a work of art.

I think it was an epidemic problem in the 1960s, but in my case, I encountered it really for the first time in connection with Andy Warhol. Here was the *Brillo Box*, and it looked just like a Brillo box, and the question was, how do you know you're a work of art when you look like something which isn't a work of art? As I said, it was like the Jesus/human being kind of problem, how do we know? At a certain moment he displays the fact that he is God, and that's the Transfiguration to some of the disciples, and Matthew describes him as "white and glistering." I love the language and used it. It was the language I thought appropriate to Duchamp's urinal, as a matter of fact, which got me in hot water with Harvard University Press, because the editor didn't want her

Savior compared to a toilet, she said. I had to struggle through that, but that was the problem: why was the urinal in that particular case a work of art? When Duchamp first saw it in the windows of J. L. Mott Ironworks it was just a urinal. It was a fascinating philosophical question, I thought, since strictly speaking there was nothing perceptual on the basis of which you could tell the two apart. *The Transfiguration of the Commonplace* undertakes to work out a kind of definition of art. I don't think it's complete, but it was as far as I could carry it, where the idea is that something is a work of art if, in the first instance, it's about something, and in the second instance, it embodies its meaning.

As it turned out, the actual Brillo carton from the supermarket is a fairly complex piece of art in its own right. The fact that it was commercial art and that I didn't think of it as art in 1981 when I published that book simply shows the snobbism, I suppose, of the times, that you drew some distinction between a work of art and commercial art. But I no longer find it necessary, and it is probably encumbering, to draw that distinction any longer.

We discovered, Karl Lüdeking, an art scholar in Germany, and I, that the Brillo box was designed by an artist, Jim Harvey. In his application for a Guggenheim, he described his day job as "part-time package designer," and his great success was this Brillo box. But there it was, a brilliant piece of rhetoric, so it seemed to me. It was about Brillo, and it proclaimed Brillo as the best thing you can get for shining aluminum, and it came in these giant-size cartons and so forth. The design is full of frenzy and red, white and blue.

The Warhol box is not a celebration of Brillo. It may be a celebration of ordinary reality, but it's certainly not about Brillo. What Warhol's work is about evades me to this day. Whatever the case, that was the problem that *The Transfiguration of the Commonplace* dealt with. At the time that I wrote it, concerned as I was with the philosophical definition of art, that is to say, looking for some set of necessary and sufficient conditions, the issue of aesthetics was not something that particularly interested me. If you take your problematic from people like Duchamp and Warhol, you're not likely to find aesthetics to be terribly important, and I bracketed it. That is to say, I never paid much attention to aesthetics in the first place because the literature of aesthetics was fairly dismal, and secondly, I couldn't find any way of fitting traditional aesthetics into the definition of art, and so that side of a philosophy of art in my case languished.

Sometime in the 1990s, I began to get interested in aesthetics, and in the last few years this has become a central preoccupation. Here is a quotation which I've found in an advertisement for a book about Dieter Roth, who was somewhat connected with Fluxus and wrote, "I hate it if I like something, if I am able to do something so that I just have to repeat it, that it should become a habit. Then I stop immediately. Also, if it threatens to become beautiful." I thought that was a pretty interesting quotation. "Threatens to become beautiful." Who is threatened by beauty? That was the question that I found myself asking. If you are somebody who makes your living selling umbrellas on the street corner of New York and somebody said, "It threatens to be a beautiful day," you could understand where beauty would be a threat. Or if you say, "My daughter threatens to be a beautiful woman," most people would rejoice, but if you're really worried about the gods being jealous and so forth and so on, you might say, "No, no, she's just an ugly thing." But most people are not threatened by beauty. I called that caliphobia, making the word up out of the Greek, caliphobia, fear of beauty. The question I really had was why caliphilia seemed to me to be the default condition for human beings. That is to say, everybody would prefer something beautiful to something ugly, and would never think of beauty as threatening. So why is it that it's become, so to speak, a condition of art that beauty is something that does threaten, and how do we account for that?

I published a book last year, as a matter of fact, called *The Abuse of Beauty,* which tries to discuss a little bit what I speculate was the art history of caliphobia, how that got to be that way, when traditionally and historically, at least since the Renaissance, beauty has been considered something that artworks should have, and that artists should aspire to and should provide. I won't go into that. It's a little tiny book and you can read the historical analysis if you've got an interest and the time. But as it turns out, there begins, these days, to be a kind of interest in beauty again, and there were this summer two conferences in the British Isles on the issue of beauty. One of them was in Cork, Ireland, where it was sponsored by the art history department at University College Cork, and the other one was in London, sponsored by the British Society for Aesthetics, and that was basically a group of philosophers. I thought it kind of interesting that geographically and at the same time, more or less, the issue of beauty, after this long neglect, should be raised by two different academic disciplines which didn't particularly share many premises. I got invited to Cork, and since I'd never been to Ireland I thought, well, here's a chance to think a little bit further about the idea of beauty from the perspective of what use are aesthetics—or *is* aesthetics; I'm never quite sure whether it's plural or singular—but what use does it have so far as the practice of art history is concerned? I think conservative writers often say, "Whatever happened to beauty? What about beauty?" When you've got art historians whose interest in art history lately, since the 1960s really, has been in identity art history, that is to say, women's art history, black art history, Asian-American art history, et cetera, I thought, well, aesthetics will probably become just like those different interests in identity—women's aesthetics, black aesthetics, Asian-American aesthetics, and so forth. If aesthetics came back it wouldn't seem to me to do much good if it got as pluralized as the practice of art history itself.

But in any case, I thought that certain ideas had emerged in *The Abuse of Beauty* that might be of some value to art historians, and I went to Cork rather than to the one in London, which I was more or less the villain of. That is to say, Arthur Danto has mostly been interested in the definition of art, but beauty, issues of aesthetics, have actually always been the point and purpose of art. I don't believe that for a moment. I don't think aesthetics has been the point and purpose of art for most of its history. There's a wonderful book by Hans Belting, the great German art historian, called *Bild und Kult*— image and cult—in which he talks about the history of the devotional image from the fall of the Roman Empire until the Renaissance—that's what art was for a thousand-odd years, and people were not concerned with whether those devotional images were beautiful or not. They were interesting to people if they performed miracles. If you could pray to the being who was present in those icons, in the devotional image, and if you made contact through prayer, then you were rewarded, and beauty would have been quite incidental and neither here nor there. I had seen a church in Germany, Vierzehnheiligen (Fourteen Holies, or Saints), and the saints are very beautiful statues. It is a Baroque church, but there are notes to Saint Barbara, to Saint Roch, and so forth, thanking the saint for making their wife's pregnancy successful, for curing fever, for doing all the things that you prayed to them to do, and I think for a long time the history of Western art was the history of objects that were powerful and that you could possibly benefit from owning, providing you treated them well. If there was beauty, it would be beauty in the frame, maybe, but the image itself was not necessarily beautiful, and when you look at some of the illustrations in Belting's book you realize that whatever they were about, they certainly weren't about aesthetics.

I don't think that anybody could reasonably say that aesthetics is what art is or has been, or that aesthetics has been the point and purpose of art. But I began to think about how, if we widen the notion of aesthetics, we begin to take into consideration the fact that mostly we've been preoccupied with a fairly narrow spectrum of the language that is used to characterize something aesthetically, when as a matter of fact, the vocabulary for aesthetics is really immensely rich. So rich that when you think about it, there is hardly a word in the language that couldn't be given an aesthetic inflection. In the canonical works of aesthetics, like Kant's *Critique of Judgment*, there will be the beautiful, the sublime—and Kant actually talks about the disgusting, and the ugly, of course, but he's interested in ugly things in the following sense, that there's nothing so ugly that it can't be beautified. Kant says the furies, disease, war, all of that can be represented beautifully, and I'm very interested in that issue of beautification. He said there's only one kind of ugliness that can't be beautified, and that is the disgusting. He doesn't talk much about it, but it's an interesting idea because beauty would be attractive, but the disgusting would be something you would want to expel, usually because disgusting is connected with things you want to spit out. Although so far as anybody has been able to follow, there is no special evolutionary reason why certain things should be disgusting and certain things not. I think most people find cockroaches disgusting, but nobody's ever eaten one, probably, and nobody knows how they really taste. So the issue of disgust is something that is interesting, but from my perspective right now not worth pursuing.

What I was interested in was, for instance, the beginning of Gerard Manley Hopkins's poem *Pied Beauty*, "Glory be to God for dappled things." "Dappled" is a descriptive term, but at the same time, obviously in Gerard Manley Hopkins's vision of the world, things that are dappled show the presence of God in a rather special way. Dappled, dumpy, drab, just to stay within the Ds, for example—you could probably find, without stretching yourself, 150 obvious aesthetic predicates.

I then began to ask myself whether there is anything that would be useful to art historians in recognizing these aesthetic qualities, and I had this idea, that actually is discussed in *The Abuse of Beauty*, of a distinction one might draw between internal and external beauty, as I call it. I call something internally beautiful if its beauty is part of the meaning of the work. I'll give you a couple of examples of that. One that interested me in *The Abuse of Beauty* was a group of paintings by Robert Motherwell, the "Elegies to the Spanish Republic," which I had always found extremely beautiful, and I began to speculate on the connection between beauty and elegy, or why beauty and death should be connected in the way they are in elegies. I thought in a case like Motherwell's the beauty is internal to the meaning of the work.

I thought equally with the Vietnam Veterans Memorial, Maya Lin's masterpiece, that the beauty was internal to the meaning of the work and indeed the function, since the function was, to use the exact language of the person who raised the money for the Vietnam Veterans Memorial, "to heal a nation." Obviously, healing still needs to be done, judging by the anti-Kerry ads lately, but Vietnam in the 1960s split the nation. It was mostly the infantrymen who raised the money for this monument. It came in little denominations—it was not a big foundation that supported the Vietnam Veterans Memorial. You had to find something that would be healing, and the beauty, it seemed to me, of that work conduced to the healing of the nation. When Maya Lin presented the sketch for the work which turned out to be the winning entry among some 1,400 submissions, her colleagues in the seminar at Yale, which was on memorial art, said that where the two wings join, that hinge, it's got to mean something. Just to describe it as a hinge gives it a meaning. It suggests that it's open like a book, for example. I thought the beauty would be there in the way in which the hinge was there; it would be part of the meaning, not just externally the case, but internally the case.

I'll give you another example, which came to me in connection with caliphobia, which is fairly familiar. Jacques-Louis David's *Marat Assassiné*, or *The Death of Marat*—the legend is that after Marat was stabbed by Charlotte Corday, the people of Paris said, "Take up thy brush, David!" I don't know whether they said anything like that, but they certainly wanted David to do something to memorialize Marat, and David came up with this incredible painting in a fairly short time. Jean-Paul Marat was slain in a bathtub. Charlotte Corday came in—she thought that if she could kill Marat, then in some way, like a suicide bomber almost, she would certainly be killed by the revolution, and that it would be a good thing. Here is Marat about to sign a petition that she presented him with. And it's not gory. You can see the blood, but if Marat looks like anything, he looks like Christ deposed. That is to say, it looks like a Deposition. It's a piece of poetry. David paints Marat not as gory, but as beautiful, unlike Mel Gibson's *The Passion of the Christ*, right? I mean that's the other side of the picture. But David depicts Marat as beautiful, as Signorelli would. So what's that beauty about, in that painting? I thought the way to think about that beauty is to establish a metaphor between Marat and Jesus. People looking at it, France being a Catholic country, would say, "Well, Jesus sacrificed himself for your sins, and Marat sacrificed himself too." In seeing that parallel, you would be moved by Marat as you would have been moved by a crucified figure, or somebody descended from a cross, and the beauty in that case would be internal to the function of the work, which was to arouse the pro-revolutionary feelings that Charlotte Corday perhaps felt that she could extinguish by getting rid of this vermin, which Marat was, I suppose, to a large degree.

At that point, there is a piece of philosophy, and I'll just sketch it, that's valuable to think about. David's painting is a little bit more complicated than the kinds of issues that I typically talk about, but the issue I began to think of was that when you're looking at a work of art, it's got the following kind of philosophical complexity: that there's a material object and there's a work, and there's a distinction between material object and work that's a little bit like the distinction between body and soul. The interesting question is, which properties of the material object are parts of the work? Those would be the properties of the material object that contribute to the meaning. I'll give you a fast example of what I've got in mind. Last year at the Guggenheim there was a wonderful exhibition of Suprematism, and it included Malevich's work of the Suprematist period, and we were able to see the first black square that Malevich painted in 1915. He did a number of black squares, but here was the black square that was the first, and to which Malevich attached immense, immense importance, immense spiritual importance and immense political importance. When you look at it—well, it's a mess, really. It's all covered with cracks. Probably Malevich didn't pay a lot of attention to problems of conservation. He probably, like the Abstract Expressionists, painted the black square without worrying about the kind of pigment that he was using, and the work probably wasn't treated terribly well at the Moscow museum that it was in, not least of all probably because Malevich was condemned as a bourgeois formalist, and why should they particularly pay attention to it? But whatever the case, Perestroika came and Malevich's paintings came out of the mothballs, and here is this painting, which is probably one of the more important, I suppose, abstract paintings in the history of the twentieth century, and it looks like hell. The question is, is that crack part of the work or is it part of the object? Obviously it's inconsistent with the principle of Suprematism that the work should be cracked. It's just a contingent fact that the material object is cracked in that way, so it's not part of the meaning of the black square. You begin to think about whether this or that physical property is part of the meaning or isn't part of the meaning of the work.

The fact that Warhol's boxes are made out of plywood is probably insignificant so far as the meaning of those works is concerned. But the fact that they're made out of plywood is deeply meaningful, I think, in the case of certain works of Donald Judd. So these are decisions that you've got to make— does it belong or doesn't it belong? I thought that for the issue of beauty, beginning with beauty but for any term used aesthetically that you care to select, the initial question is, is it part of the object or part of the work? If it is part of the work, it contributes to the meaning. That would be a valuable distinction for art historians to make, to find out which properties were meaningful and why they were meaningful, and I thought that the *Marat Assassiné* would have been a good example of that.

The concern in Cork, the concern of the sponsors of the conference, was that they wanted aesthetics but they didn't want to bring back what they dismissed as art appreciation. I guess I can understand that. They thought they were doing something more important than what is done by typical docents in museums—"Notice this, notice that," and so forth. My interest is in what one might call an aesthetics of meaning rather than an aesthetics of form, and I thought the aesthetics of meaning might make a contribution— even if you're divided in the way that I suggested art history is, through different kinds of identity art history—it could be a valuable tool to penetrate when something is meaningful and how it is meaningful. So those are the kinds of questions I've been working with lately. Thanks.

2005

I am Arthur Danto, and my main kind of work is philosophy, which I've written for a long time. I've always had a number or friends who are artists and I've had a great interest in art, but no interest whatever in the philosophy of art until roughly the middle 1960s, when art suddenly revealed a philosophical face, to me at any rate, and I began to write analytical pieces on the concept. Publishing *The Transfiguration of the Commonplace* in 1981 led to my getting invited to write for people other than philosophers. Up to that point, I only had a philosophical audience, but after *The Transfiguration* appeared I began to write for places like the *SoHo News*, and ultimately *The Nation* magazine. I was invited to be their art critic. I'd never written a line of art criticism, nor had I thought of it.

This evening, what I want mainly to talk about is an exhibition in which, in a certain sense, *The Nation* and philosophy both play a certain role. I'm not somebody who's deeply interested in curating but occasionally somebody prevails on me to try it, and in this case I had some incentive to do it because the exhibition that I thought of was connected with the anniversary of 9/11. Occasionally, as a philosopher, I think about possible exhibitions, but they're not the kind that would ordinarily be deeply interesting to anybody to come and look at. For example, *The Transfiguration* begins with an exhibition which I'll very briefly describe. It's based on a joke of Søren Kierkegaard, the Danish philosopher, who was very witty, and particularly witty writing about art. It's a monochrome joke, but monochrome painting before 1915 really existed only as jokes and chiefly in philosophical books like Hegel's *The Phenomenology of Spirit* and in this book of Kierkegaard called *Either/Or*. And the joke goes as follows: a man is commissioned to do a painting for a church, and when it's unveiled it's a red square, and he is asked, "Well, what's the painting about?" He replies, "It's about the Jews crossing the Red Sea. They've gotten to the other side. The waters have closed over the forces of Pharaoh and calm has been restored." And Kierkegaard says, "My life's like that painting. A single mood. A color. A profound kind of boredom." I thought, well that would make an interesting painting in its own right, so I put next to my imagined piece of historical painting, *The Jews Crossing the Red Sea*, another painting looking exactly like it called *Kierkegaard's Mood*, which is a piece of psychological portraiture. At that point I began to imagine a lot of red squares—for example, one a piece of Moscow landscape that I called *Red Square*; then a red tablecloth—an imagined painting by Matisse; there was also a religious painting—*The Red Dust*, based on the Buddhist thought that the Samsara world and the Nirvana world are one and the same; and then a few more. I included one which has an art historical interest, because I'm imagining that it was grounded by Giorgione in red lead, on which he intended to paint a *sacra conversazione*, but he never got around to it. Still and all, I put it in my exhibition as something that isn't a work of art, but looks like a work of art, or at least as much like the other works of art as they looked like one another. And then I knew a rebellious artist who says to me, "Look, I'm going to paint a red square and it's not going to mean anything. Will you put it in your show?" And I say, "Sure. Your square means nothing." And then finally, I've got a red square which is just a red square, just a piece of painted plywood. So you've got ultimately eight paintings. They all look alike but they belong to different genres, and they have different meanings and each one calls for a different interpretation.

The Transfiguration of the Commonplace endeavors to set out a theory of art, and my feeling was that if it's going to be an interesting theory of art, it's got to be able to cover cases like that. Anybody can write a theory of art about the Sistine ceiling but you've got to be able to get a philosophy of art that both explains why some of these are works of art and some of them aren't, and why they're different works of art, not just, as logicians say, *solo numero*, but actually different works of art coming out of different impulses. Something I owed to Kierkegaard. If I were to put an exhibition of that sort on, people would get pretty angry walking in and seeing a lot of red squares, but my ambition actually is to see an exhibition a lot like that. For instance, Barbara and I were at the Bonnefanten Museum in Maastricht and the director of the museum has an extraordinary painting by Pieter Bruegel called *The Census at Bethlehem*, and he said Bruegel did thirteen *Census at Bethlehem*s. And I thought if there is any show I'd like to see, it would be all thirteen Bruegels of *The Census at Bethlehem*. I think finally I would really get some understanding of what went into a single Bruegel painting if I had them all.

The exhibition that I'm actually in the process of curating and will open soon, may, as a matter of fact, affect people a little bit as though it's a philosophical exhibition ["The Art of 9/11," Apex Art, New York City, September 7–October 15, 2005]. Though it has a philosophical justification, it comes out of experiences that people had with 9/11, including us. The day of 9/11, I was supposed to have a public conversation with an artist, a photographer I admire a lot, Joseph Bartscherer. It was to have preceded the opening reception for his show at the Davis Museum at Wellesley College, and, interestingly enough, given the events of the day, the work on view was an installation called *Obituary*. Joseph had been collecting front pages of the *New York Times* since the early 1990s, the criterion being whether an obituarial photograph appears on the front page. He felt that he would learn a lot about the culture if he could figure out why certain people's obituaries appear on the front page, and when they do, whether they get a photograph, and then where the photograph itself appears. I learned a lot thinking about those obituarial photographs—where they're placed, and what other photographs are there. For example, when William Clinton's mother died, her photograph was certainly on the front page, but below the fold, as they say—it wasn't up toward the top. And then there was, juxtaposed with it, a photograph of Nancy Kerrigan, who had just been incapacitated from skating by Tonya Harding, and here was a picture of Nancy Kerrigan, a portrait of her—a very, very pretty girl and a wonderful skater. But that was the first early edition. By the time the later editions of the *Times* came out, there was, instead, a photograph of Nancy Kerrigan in pain. She'd been struck and the photographer got her when she was bending over to nurse her knee, and it looks like she's mourning for Mrs. Clinton. That is to say, that was the image the photographic editor of the *Times* decided belonged on the front page. That project of Joseph's is something that has caused me ever since to pay a great deal of attention to the front page. But the conversation with Joseph never transpired. We were supposed to take a morning train. I looked, as I always do, at the headlines on Yahoo and I saw the headline, "Two Planes Crash into the World Trade Center in Apparent Terrorist Attack." I instantly thought it was a hoax, went to Channel One, which in

New York, if anything's happening, tells you exactly what it is, and there we saw it and that was that for the rest of the day. There were no trains running, or anything else. But in the middle of the day, how this happened I have no idea, a telephone call came through from somebody who claimed to be writing something for the *New York Times*, and he says, "What's the art world going to do about this?" I thought, "Nothing."

Basically, I couldn't think that anybody—any artist I knew—would be doing anything except what I was doing. That is to say, if they weren't at the towers, they were going to be looking at television and at the crowds in the street. I learned two things from the World Trade Center event, that ordinary people are capable of great acts of heroism, and that ordinary people, again, respond to events like that with art. I'd be very glad not to know either of those things, but those are two things I found out, because as soon as we walked outside—we don't live near the World Trade Center, we live on the Upper West Side of Manhattan—but when we went out, our neighborhood was covered with vernacular shrines, little shrines that people placed deliberately on stairs, along window sills. At Strauss Park, not far from us, there were these shrines, and I've given them a great deal of thought, the vernacular shrines, and I thought that no artist would've been able to respond more appropriately to the event than quite ordinary people who perhaps knew nothing about art. I'd like myself to understand what the psychology of that response was.

Not long after 9/11, I was invited to give a lecture at the Maryland Institute, and I was taken to see the faculty show, and a person I had known before who's the dean down there, Leslie King Hammond, had built a shrine much more elaborate than what one found on 106th Street and Broadway, but still, I thought rather a remarkable work, and probably not a work which would have been made by Leslie or maybe any artist before the experience of the vernacular shrines. I was deeply impressed with that work.

In the course of time, people began to talk to me about art they had made in response to 9/11, and I'll give you just a couple of examples because they're kind of interesting. Audrey Flack, who's an artist I like and a very feisty woman, naturally rushed down to Ground Zero to try and be of help, but when she got there she realized that everything was too well organized for her to make a contribution, and she tried to be of help but couldn't, and then she said she was seized really with a need to go to Montauk Point and to paint boats. Just to paint boats. It was obviously something that was a need, one might call it a spiritual need, and Audrey went out and she did these paintings. I thought that these were paintings done in a spirit of ritual, almost. They looked like quite ordinary watercolors, although Audrey's a gifted artist, but I thought, here's something that's invisible, practically. Nobody looking at one of those would know it was anything except a watercolor that somebody did by the side of the sea, by a dock.

Another instance was two works by Lucio Pozzi. Lucio told me that the day after the event, or maybe two days after, he got a phone call from a friend in Italy, who said, "Well, I suppose there's no possibility of making art now." And Lucio said, "On the contrary, I'm painting a picture at this very moment." The picture he was painting was actually a watercolor, which was a copy of a painting that was reproduced in a catalog of his, and when he finished that he made another copy, and then when he was finished with that copy, he went out and he took photographs—bang, bang, bang, bang, like that—of smoke on Mulberry Street. His studio was on Mulberry Street. He made these into a little pamphlet which he sent to his friends, and it doesn't look like anything. The title of the pamphlet is *Something/Nothing*, meaning that it looks like gray monochrome photographs, but in fact they're photographs of smoke, as smoke took a long time to clear. I thought at that time that if I ever did a show, I'd like to have both Audrey's paintings and Lucio's work, both the photographs and the watercolors. On the anniversary of 9/11, this is what I thought about—those photographs. I got this passage from Wittgenstein—this is from a text of his not usually read by people. It's "Remarks on Frazer's *Golden Bough*," and it has always moved me. He says, "Recall that after Schubert's death his brother cut some of Schubert's scores into small pieces and gave such pieces, consisting of a few bars, to his favorite pupils. This act, as a sign of piety, is *just as* understandable . . . as keeping the scores untouched, accessible to no one. And if Schubert's brother had burned the scores, that too would be understandable as an act of piety." That idea of understanding, *verständlich*, is what impresses me in that statement of Wittgenstein's because it makes clear that any given culture is going to have certain practices for which there are rules in order to meet the major contingencies of life. So that if there's death there's going to be weeping, there's going to be tearing of hair, rending of garments, and so forth and so on. But we also would understand it if somebody did something different, something that had never been done before, but you say, "Yes, I understand that. I can understand that."

It's as though everybody carries around a kind of theory of the culture like a theory of language, where the theory of language enables you to both produce and understand sentences of a kind which have never been produced or understood before. For example, you've never heard any of these sentences this evening, and it's through the work of Noam Chomsky that we know that about language, but I think something like that's true of culture, and it's true of many things. What is it to be a kind person? To be a kind person is to do kind things, but what are they? Somebody says, "I'd like to be a kind person," and I say, "Okay, this is what you've got to do. You've got to help crippled people across the streets maybe. And if you see a horse, it's a good idea to carry some water." But that's not what it is to be a kind person. A kind person is somebody who does the right thing without there being a rule for it, and we do that all the time. Or making love, or actually showing consideration, these are dispositions that human beings have, and I think that these cultural moments that Wittgenstein describes here are things that we understand as being the right thing to do. They're inconsistent with one another, but each of them is appropriate.

On the first anniversary of 9/11, *The Nation* decided to publish an anniversary issue, and Katrina vanden Heuvel, the editor, asked if I'd write a piece on 9/11 and art, and I wrote about these artists I just mentioned, but I also got interested in what other artists might have done. What had they done— people that I knew? It wasn't in any way a piece of sociological investigation or anything like that. But I wrote Cindy Sherman, who's a pretty good pal, and here's what she wrote. She said, "I'm fine, though it's hard to think of what kind of work to make at this point other than decorative, escapist, or abstract. I suppose I'll explore one or all of these things." You can't imagine a work by Cindy Sherman that's any of those things, decorative or abstract or escapist.

Then I decided more recently to make an exhibition of this work for Apex Art if I could track down enough of it, so I wrote Cindy and I said, "You remember this exchange we had, this correspondence—what did you do in fact?" She described to me two photographs that she'd done, one of which I'd actually seen at a museum in Arizona, of a woman in a kerchief, and it looked like something done in the 1930s, some Stakhanovite poster, almost, of a woman— not like anything that Cindy had ever done before. She also said to me that the clown photographs that she showed in 2004 at Metro Pictures were responses to 9/11. She felt she wouldn't have done them without that. So, okay. In 2002 I had seen an exhibition of Ursula von Rydingsvard's up at the Neuberger Museum at SUNY Purchase, and there was a huge thing by Ursula—she does nothing but huge things, as you know, but still and all—here was this strange piece called *Mama Build Me a Fence*. Ursula has an extraordinary history, and I was sure that piece came out of 9/11. I wrote her and I said, "Did 9/11, as a matter of fact, give rise to . . . ?" And she said yes. It turned out this work was one for the 9/11 show, too. And Robert Zakanitch was another. I wrote Robert, who was a member of the Pattern and Decoration movement of the late 1970s, and a painter I really love. I said, "Well, what did you do, if anything, in response to 9/11?" He said, "I painted lace." I wrote, "Why?" He said, "Basically, it's about restoring balance in the firmament. They're not about war and about being a victim, to both of which I am opposed." Well, his impulse was to do that. So I thought I had a fairly interesting show. Mary Miss did a beautiful work called *Moving Perimeter: A Wreath for Ground Zero*. She felt there should be a mourning zone around that place. She designed that piece and then ran into terrible resistance from the Municipal Art Society and the Ground Zero people and so forth. But the design is quite handsome. So there'll be a lot of works in this show which don't look like 9/11 art at all. That is to say, they don't look they're responses, but as Wittgenstein says, we understand how somebody could do that, or would do that, or would think that. I've asked the artists each to write some kind of a statement explaining to people what they had in mind, and the statements that they sent me in letters are pretty interesting.

I'll finish up very quickly. The artist in my first exhibition, the imagined show of red paintings, who said, "I'm just going to do a painting, a red square, which doesn't mean anything," that's an artist named Jeffrey Lohn, who was a student of mine when I was teaching at the University of California in San Diego as a visiting professor. He was a wonderful student to have a dialogue with, and I put him in *The Transfiguration of the Commonplace* under the name J, and we've carried on a discussion ever since. Jeffrey, not long after 9/11, began to photograph the photographs that everybody remembers— "Have you seen this man?" and a description and so forth. He photographed them each day, as the rain and the wind and the dirt of the city reduced them just to scraps of paper, a kind of second death, which was very, very powerful. Then Barbara did a piece that I wanted in the show because, like most New Yorkers, we felt that the blue lights that came on for the anniversary of 9/11 probably were the best memorial that anybody had ever thought of. In fact, we went down to Apex Art to see the lights from the roof. The gallery—the whole building, in fact—is owned by an exceptionally interesting person named Stephen Rand, and it seemed appropriate to have Barbara's painting of the two columns of light as chronologically the last thing in the show. So I think that the value of the show is that, although each of these people is an exceptionally interesting artist, these are works which were produced as responses to an extraordinary event, and I think they go some distance in the same way in which the shrines went to explain how people use art, sometimes in extreme situations, as acts of piety—let's use Wittgenstein's expression. Thanks.

2006

I'm Arthur Danto. I write a column of art criticism for *The Nation* magazine, and I've also spent most of my mature life as a professor of philosophy at Columbia University. I'm now emeritus. It's in the latter capacity that I'd like to talk a little bit this evening. And primarily, one talks about what one's thinking about at the time one's doing the talking, at least that's been the case with me.

Lately, I've been much preoccupied by the fact that my first book on the philosophy of art is twenty-five years old. I called the book *The Transfiguration of the Commonplace*. People who were interested in the book told me that it was twenty-five years old, and there'll be a certain number of celebratory occasions to mark that passage. In my profession, that consists in people lining up and telling you in a fairly formal way what's wrong with what you've done, and you responding as best you can. The truth of the matter is that I hadn't really looked at this book since I turned in the last set of proofs. So I brought a copy up to begin thinking, what am I going to say about it on these occasions?

I was not really somebody who specialized in any way in the philosophy of art, which was by and large a good thing, because I couldn't really see what the connection was between the canonical works in the history of the philosophy of art and anything that was happening around me in New York. I had a lot of friends who were artists and I felt a tremendous disconnect between what graduate students were required to study in a field called aesthetics or philosophy of art and what you were likely to see in the really interesting galleries that were around. And I think even fairly literate artists also found it difficult to see what the point of the philosophy of art was. There was a famous episode at Woodstock, New York, in 1952, when the American Society of Aesthetics organized a conference involving some aestheticians and a certain number of artists, and on one of the panels, Barnett Newman made the famous *mot* that aesthetics is to artists what ornithology is to the birds. I felt bad about that afterward because a teacher who was rather beloved was on that panel, Susanne K. Langer. She wrote a very interesting and important book called *Philosophy in a New Key*, which was really about the philosophy of art. I took her classes, but if anybody said, "So listen, Arthur, what's this got to do with what's happening at Betty Parsons or what's happening at the Sidney

Janis Gallery," I would have been hard pressed to say, "Well, this is what it has to do with those things." There seemed, as I say, to be that kind of chasm.

I think 1952 must have been a remarkable year when the zeitgeist was concentrated in Woodstock, New York, because it was in Maverick Concert Hall in Woodstock that there was the premiere of John Cage's *4'33"*, played by David Tudor, which, as everybody here certainly knows, consisted of all the noises, the circumambient noises that were made after Tudor closed the lid of the piano. There were three movements, and all that you heard was what was going on, the breathing, the automobiles passing, a radio, perhaps in the distance a dog barking, and then that was it. Cage, in that performance, in that piece, was primarily interested in what turned out to be the kind of problem that really was, I thought, philosophical, namely, how do we distinguish musical sounds from sounds *tout court*, and why shouldn't we be able to make music out of anything—anything, really anything auditory. And largely, Cage's ideas had a Zen quality about them. Cage attended Dr. Suzuki's lectures at my university, and various members of the art world made their way to Columbia to listen to Dr. Suzuki in those years on the seventh floor of Philosophy Hall. The elevator would open and out would come a group of people who clearly didn't belong in the philosophy department, looking lost. I would say, "Dr. Suzuki is *there*," and they would listen to him, as I did and, in fact, I got a great deal out of what Dr. Suzuki had to say.

Two years ago, I wrote an essay for Jackie Baas and Mary Jane Jacob's book *Buddha Mind in Contemporary Art*, an essay that I called "Upper West Side Buddhism," and a lot of the ideas that I got as an Upper West Side Buddhist for a very short period turned into the philosophy of art. Why not make music out of anything was echoed by Robert Rauschenberg—why not make art out of anything—in his catalog entry for "Sixteen Americans," the great exhibition that Dorothy Miller put on at the Museum of Modern Art in 1959. Rauschenberg, Johns, Ellsworth Kelly, Frank Stella and Louise Nevelson are among the ones I particularly remember. And one had the sense, at that point, that some deep change, really, was taking place in the art world. You can get a sense of the depth of the change if you read about John Canaday's letter to Dorothy Miller. A few days after that exhibition opened he said,

"For my money, these are the sixteen artists most slated for oblivion," and the woman who was the art critic for the *Herald Tribune*, Emily Genauer, was equally impatient with that kind of art. But I was deeply interested in it and, in a sense, deeply interested in Stella's remark, which has a philosophical aura about it, in which he says, "What you see is what you see."

Because the problem, really, as it was coming up, was that there had begun to appear works of art that looked entirely like objects that by common consent weren't works of art, and if what you see is what you see, then how can you tell the difference between them? That seemed to me to be, for the first time, a revelation of what one might call the philosophical face of art. One began to see why philosophers had, really from the beginning of philosophy, been preoccupied with some questions in the philosophy of art, and you can even see the history of art as a history of efforts to define the artwork. But throughout that long period of twenty-five hundred years, you had no difficulty, for the most part, identifying which were the works of art, because they were singular objects. That is to say, you could recognize them in the way in which you could recognize a giraffe or you could recognize a rose, you could learn the meaning of artworks by ostension, like, "These are the artworks, these are the giraffes, these are the roses." When you've gotten to the point where the work of art turns out to be really indiscernible from something that isn't a work of art, then the question is, how do you teach the meaning of a term like "work of art," and how do you tell, how do you recognize works of art?

That was the problem that I thought I wanted to address philosophically. But this book, *The Transfiguration of the Commonplace*, came at the end of a sequence of books. I had made up my mind, as an analytical philosopher, that I was going to write a systematic study of analytical philosophy in five volumes. I'd gotten a pretty clear idea of what I wanted those volumes to take up and how the internal logic of those volumes should go. I took, as the central concept that I was to deal with, the concept of representation. And my first book, which was called *Analytical Philosophy of History*, was about narrative representation, and then there were two books of a fairly narrow sort that followed that, *Analytical Philosophy of Knowledge* and then *Analytical Philosophy of Action*, in which I talk about representations and reality. And then finally, I wrote this book. By that time, I was a bit fed up with analytical philosophy and I wanted at least to call it something else, and the title *The Transfiguration of the Commonplace* I encountered in a novel of Muriel Spark's, *The Prime of Miss Jean Brodie*. I adored Muriel Spark as a writer, and the central figure, a Glasgow girl named, allegorically, I suppose, Sandy Stranger, who's a rake and no better than she needs to be, winds up a nun, and her name is Sister Helena of the Transfiguration. And she writes a book called *The Transfiguration of the Commonplace*, which gets to be a very successful book as it turns out. People pester Sister Helena, asking her questions about this book. She'd like to stop answering those questions and would like very much to lead a life of contemplation and devotion, but her Mother Superior feels this is her penance, I guess, for writing a book, and so she has to keep encountering people.

I didn't think it was so bad, actually, to write a book called *The Transfiguration of the Commonplace* that people wanted to know about, but lately I've acquired a certain sympathy for Sister Helena, as my book has gone through not merely different editions, but a great many different translations. You find yourself having to give interviews, answer an awful lot of questions about the book, actually write prefaces to the Portuguese edition or the Chinese edition or the Japanese edition and so forth and so on. So I've become sympathetic, as I say, with her. But I wrote Muriel Spark and said, "There's no indication of what the book was about, and could you tell me how you conceived of it?" She said, "I conceived of it as about art as I practice it." And I thought, well, that was a wonderful answer, better, I suppose, than I could have anticipated. What the transfiguration of the commonplace was, I suppose, that you take a commonplace girl from the streets of Glasgow, who's got a certain wickedness and certain sexual drives, and then she's transfigured into Sister Helena of the Transfiguration. She's still the same person, but she's now been transfigured into something quite out of the ordinary, just by being a nun, I thought. So I felt that that was very close to what I was after. That is to say, commonplace is a beautiful word and artists had begun, in some way, to transfigure. Transfigure, that concept that comes up in the Gospel of Matthew, where Christ reveals his divinity with these prophets on either side of him, and he's "white and glistering," as the Bible says.

I'm deeply moved by that idea of transfiguration, because it occurred to me that the problem of a work of art and something that wasn't a work of art, where they looked exactly alike, was pretty much like the Jesus/ordinary guy kind of problem. You say, well, exactly what makes you a god? Exactly what is that like? It was easy enough to establish Christ's humanity. The paintings of the Circumcision do that—the first blood that's shed at the Circumcision demonstrates the humanity that is there. But how do you establish the other part of it, that he's a human being who happens to be a god? You could do it with a symbol like a halo, but how, in fact, could anybody tell? In any case, that was the problem that I began to solve, and reading the book over, I realize how I was finding my way in the dark. I'd like just to read the beginning because I don't think that there's another book quite like it that begins anything like this. Maybe some of you've read it, but then you'll pardon this:

> Let us consider a painting once described by the Danish wit, Søren Kierkegaard. It was a painting of the Israelites crossing the Red Sea. Looking at it, one would have seen something very different from what a painting with that subject would have led one to expect, were one to imagine, for example, what an artist like Poussin or Altdorfer would have painted: troops of people, in various postures of panic, bearing the burdens of their dislocated lives, and in the distance the horsed might of the Egyptian forces bearing down. Here, instead, was a square of red paint, the artist explaining that "the Israelites had already crossed over, and the Egyptians were drowned." Kierkegaard comments that the result of his life is like that painting. All the spiritual turmoil, the father cursing God on the heath, the rupture with Regina Olsen, the inner search for Christian meaning, the sustained polemics of an agonized soul, meld in the end, as in the echoes of the Marabar Caves, into "a mood, a single color."
>
> So next to Kierkegaard's described painting, let us place another, exactly like it, this one, let us suppose, by a Danish portraitist, who with immense psychological penetration, has produced a work called *Kierkegaard's Mood*.

I proceeded to generate an imaginary exhibition consisting of red squares. The next painting was a piece of Moscow landscape called *Red Square*. And next to that, a red Minimalist painting. And then a red square by Matisse, called *Red Tablecloth*, a very reduced version, you might say, of *Le Dessert*. And next to that, a religious painting called *The Red Dust*, learning, as we have, from the Buddhist seers that the Nirvana world and the Samsara world are identical. And then I put a red painting—well, it's not a painting, in fact. It's got an art-historical interest, though, because it's red lead, and it was grounded by Giorgione, who didn't live long enough to paint the *sacra conversazione*. And then, just a red board. I thought, you've got enough to work with there. You've got a historical painting, a psychological portrait, you've got a religious painting, you've got a landscape, you've got a still life. And then you've got something which isn't a painting, but the paint was put on by an artist, and then you've just got a red square. And imagine an exhibition like that, where a catalogue for it is fairly monotonous. Everything looks exactly alike, but what you see is what you see. And they're all, on the other hand, different and belong to different genres.

And that was the problem that I set out to solve in the book. My inspiration obviously was Warhol, and in particular, his 1964 exhibition of the industrial shipping cartons, which were indiscernible—what you see— from the shipping cartons themselves. And so how do you tell the difference when the differences have to be invisible? *Have* to be invisible. The solution to the problem, at least in the case of visual art, *has* to take into account that what you're looking for can't be seen. And then I stepped out from there. The structure of the book—and I'd probably better conclude—is like a classical Socratic dialogue. I'm looking for a couple of necessary conditions, that is to say, conditions necessary for something to be a work of art. The book, in about 200 pages, finesses out two or maybe two and a half necessary conditions which will yield something like a definition of a work of art. But it's a very austere definition, and applies to the most unprepossessing works of art I could find. That was the beauty of the art world of the 1960s, everything was unprepossessing, really, and what was interesting and deep and moving about it was that it was unprepossessing. I wanted to find something that fit those works and then would fit everything else. But it was going to leave out, obviously, things that, since they belong to works of art, but don't belong to all works of art, couldn't be part of the definition. And so you wound up with something that leaves out everything interesting to anybody but a philosopher. But it was a definition that holds water. And what has interested me in my experiences in the art world ever since is how that definition has enabled me to practice criticism without any agenda whatsoever. It's simple enough to identify a work of art. The two conditions were that it's got to have a meaning—it's got to be about something—and then the meaning has got to be embodied in the work.

Lately I've begun to feel my way into the philosophy of art that begins with, at least in modern times, the philosophy of Kant, which I think we've been distracted from, the philosophy of art which begins late in the *Critique of Judgment*. Up to that point, Kant talks about beauty, which has no application, it just has no application to most of what I was looking at in the 1960s and '70s, let alone the '80s, let alone today. So I've been thinking about aesthetics, and that I was easily able to eliminate. But Kant offers a very interesting philosophy of art around Section 49 of the *Critique of Judgment,* and lately I've been trying to, as it were, shake hands with Kant and say, "You were on the right track all along." Thanks very much.

2007

Hi, I'm Arthur Danto, and I'm from the margins of the art world, really, because my true calling is as a philosopher, and that's been my livelihood as well. Last summer when I was here, I talked a little bit about a book I'd published twenty-five years earlier, the title of which was *The Transfiguration of the Commonplace*. I didn't know that it had been published twenty-five years ago. I didn't do that computation. If anybody asked me, "Well, when was it published?" I could have told them, but I didn't think, "This is twenty-five years." But other people found out about it, or knew about it, or counted on it happening, and so they began to write and congratulate me, and I thought I'd better reread the book, because I hadn't looked at it for a very long time— well, twenty-five years, to be exact. So I thought, here I am coming up to Kippy's, so I'll talk a little bit about the book. But part of the consequence of it being twenty-five years old, which is an auspicious anniversary, was that there were several conferences organized to discuss the book, and one of them I'll talk a little bit about, because it's so twenty-first century.

This was an online conference on the book organized by three young philosophers, one from the University of Chicago, one from Vanderbilt, one from Tel Aviv. They put out a call for papers and got a big response, so they raised the money, and I agreed, naturally, to participate. There were about twenty-five papers, plus a couple of keynote essays and so forth, and the way it worked was that they would release a couple of papers, and then people would respond to the papers and respond to one another, and then they'd release another couple of papers, and then there would be more of this commentary, until by the time all the papers had been released there was quite an extraordinary dialogue that accompanied it. I didn't comment, because I felt it was appropriate for me to answer directly everybody who submitted a paper. People put a fair amount of work into those papers, and so I wrote all these responses. If you're interested, it's still floating around cyberspace, and if you type in "Danto conference" you can probably find it. I thought I'd talk a little bit about, for those of you who may have read the book, some of the things I learned from the conversation as it unfurled.

I didn't start out to be a philosopher of art or an aesthetician or anything like that. I started to do philosophy in kind of a golden age of analytical thinking, and I really loved analytical philosophy, and I had no interest in writing philosophically about art, chiefly because I didn't see how to do it. But I had a lesson from the art world itself, mainly through Pop and Minimalism in the middle 1960s. I've written frequently enough about an extraordinary show—I suppose if that hadn't happened, I never would have written anything in philosophy about art, that is to say, never written anything about art. I wouldn't have gotten into art criticism if I hadn't written *The Transfiguration of the Commonplace* itself. I'm referring to that legendary show in which Warhol displayed about one hundred *Brillo Boxes*— well, nobody knows exactly how many boxes, and there were also Kellogg's corn flakes boxes, Mott's apple juice boxes, Del Monte peach half boxes, Heinz tomato ketchup boxes, and so forth and so on. Nobody's entirely sure of any of that, but there is a catalogue raisonné of Warhol's work that makes a stab at least of estimating the numbers. And there are some bills of sale and so forth. The *Brillo Boxes* were really the star of the show. I got terribly interested in a question that suddenly did seem to me to be a philosophical question, namely, why were these works of art? I was perfectly glad to consider them works of art. They excited me actually as works of art, but why were they works of art, when things that looked just like them, namely, the ordinary Brillo boxes that were workaday containers for shipping Brillo—why weren't they works of art?

I wrote an essay called "The Artworld," and I think that what I had in mind at the time—this was 1964—was a political question, essentially. And by the art world I meant the world of artworks, a kind of community of artworks. I thought, if you're an artwork, you have a really interesting existence. That is to say, people pay a lot of attention to you. You go for a good bit of money if you get sold. You have rights. You've got privileges. If somebody injures you, it's considered vandalism, and so forth. So that's a very exalted kind of existence. But here are these other things, Brillo boxes, which don't have any rights or privileges, and you can destroy them with impunity and nobody pays any attention to that. And 1964—that was the Freedom Summer, when everybody trooped to Mississippi to register black voters and to see that they were re-enfranchised, really. They were enfranchised, but to get them registered as voters. I was really interested in the question of enfranchisement. How do you get to be an artwork? You say, "Well, these are made of cardboard, and these are made of plywood," and you say, "Well, yeah, but these guys are black, and these guys are white," but what difference does that make? What difference does cardboard and plywood make and so forth?

At any rate, one of the questions that came up in the critical discussion about my book was this. The person said I'd really misconstrued the show entirely, that it was an installation, and I was talking about it as though it was a conjunction of individual works, and if I had seen it, the writer said, as an installation, then I might not have raised these kinds of questions. Maybe I would have, maybe I wouldn't have. But the truth of the matter is, it seemed an interesting question. I wasn't sure exactly how to answer it. How do you tell the difference between an entity consisting of individual boxes and then simply a conjunction of boxes? I thought that really had to be answered. A conference on the *Brillo Box* had been held at Nuremberg in Germany, and some philosophers and a few artists were invited. One of the artists was Gerard Malanga, who was Warhol's right-hand guy, and Gerard gave a talk about the origins of the *Brillo Box*, and he said some interesting things to which I hadn't paid a lot of attention at the time. In the light of this particular question, I remembered what Gerard had said. I think the original impulse was to take a lot of Brillo boxes, just Brillo boxes ordered from the factory. These, it turned out, didn't have the look, when they were stacked up, that Warhol wanted. What Warhol wanted was very uniform repetition of the kind that you see on the supermarket shelves, and a bunch of the cartons didn't give that effect. He was, in other words, looking for an effect that the real thing wouldn't yield, and so he had the boxes that he used fabricated. He had Gerard go to a carpenter to build two or three hundred boxes of different sizes for the different products, and so forth. And you could see what he was getting at, in that case—he wanted sharp edges and sharp corners. And an artist at that time, if what they wanted was really sharp edges and really sharp corners, they had them fabricated. Donald Judd did that. Donald Judd probably thought, "I can't make corners like a machine shop can make corners, so I'm going to have my things done by a machine shop because that's the effect I want." And that, I think, is an argument for an installation. You wanted an almost futuristic installation of Brillo boxes, which, had they been the real thing—the readymade, so to speak, wouldn't have given that effect because they were too soft.

They were sold one by one by one. Nobody was buying a dozen or anything like that. In fact, they didn't sell very well at all, but Warhol wanted them to sell and thought they would sell, and in my recollection, people were walking around carrying single *Brillo Box*es, but there were a lot left over. A lot. A Toronto art dealer tried to take about eighty of them—that's a lot left over from a show of one hundred—and take them to his gallery. The customs wouldn't let them through, except as merchandise. He said, "No, this is sculpture," and they said, "For us, it's merchandise," and so they consulted the director of the National Gallery of Canada, who was an expert in sculpture, and asked him, "Is this sculpture?" and he said, "No. No, definitely not sculpture." So the customs people said, "Well, there's your expert and he says it's not sculpture, so it's merchandise." Ultimately they never got to Toronto.

Nobody bought Warhol in those years, although the other day the *Green Car Crash* went for, as I discovered in the paper today, nearly twice what just today a Raphael went for. Raphael went for $37 million; Warhol was $71 million. That's pretty close to twice as much. But the reason I mention that was, after I published "The Artworld," the idea of art world was misread by a colleague, a man named George Dickie at the University of Chicago, who thought that what I meant by the art world was not a community of artworks, which is what I did mean, but a group of people who decide whether something is art or not. He thought that something gets to be an artwork— which is an answer to the enfranchisement question—when the art world decides. And you say, "Well, do they meet? Where do they get together?" and so forth. But the evidence of the Canadian expert on sculpture counts heavily against the theory of the art world as a social body that makes judgments as to what is an artwork and what isn't. I didn't like that particular theory at all, but then I realized I was going to have to do some work, because I didn't really know how to answer the question that I initially raised about why it is an artwork and something pretty much like it isn't an artwork.

I had kind of a mantra that came from the philosopher Wittgenstein in connection with actions, like raising an arm. Wittgenstein had this thought. "Well, if from the fact that I raise my arm, you subtract the fact that my arm went up, what's left over?" I think Wittgenstein really wanted to say there's nothing to raising an arm that isn't just an arm going up, but that seems like a bad piece of philosophy, or at least it did to me. So there is some solution to that problem, but I thought, it's interesting to me that there's a comparable mantra for the work of art problem, namely, if from the fact that something's a work of art, you subtract the physical object of which the work of art consists, what's left over? So you solve for X in the action case, you solve for Y in the art case. And then, you can do the same thing in the theory of knowledge, where from the fact that somebody knows that X, you subtract the fact that he believes that X, what's left over? What turns belief into knowledge? You've got three parallel structures there, and I thought that was deeply interesting, more interesting than trying to solve the problem all by itself. So I wrote a series of books, one devoted to the arm raising problem, one devoted to the theory of knowledge problem, and I tried to solve for X and Y, and then when I'd gotten those out of the way, I was ready to write *The Transfiguration of the Commonplace*, which was to be the fourth volume in a five-volume systematic work on analytical philosophy.

I knew that I was going to have to give a definition of art that would hold water. And that's what *The Transfiguration of the Commonplace* really is. It's got the structure of a Platonic dialogue, in the sense that Socrates and his friends get engaged in questions like what justice is or what friendship is or what courage is and so forth, and then they try to answer the question by somebody offering a definition, somebody trying to defeat the definition, and then, bit by bit, you arrive at something that looks like it might be a definition, and then you say, well, that's what justice is or that's what knowledge is or that's what friendship is or that's what love is, or whatever.

I managed to come up with two necessary conditions. That is to say, I really thought they were necessary conditions. The first one was that it's got to be about something. It's got to represent something. It's got to have a meaning. But for reasons that wouldn't be worth going into here because they're agonizing, I said, "I need a second necessary condition." And then I came up with this idea that there are many things that have meaning, but the interesting thing about artworks is that they embody their meanings. That was a more complicated condition, but I think it held up. So I came up with the thought that for X to be a work of art, X has to have a meaning, and embody it. But different objects will embody their meaning in different kinds of ways, and the meaning picks out the properties of the physical object that consist in the embodiment of that meaning. So what meaning it's got is really invisible. You can't tell usually by looking at it, but I think probably everything that's interesting in philosophy is invisible.

That was what *The Transfiguration of the Commonplace* was about. It served me very well in doing art criticism, when I started to write for *The Nation*—it was because of *The Transfiguration* that I got asked to become an art critic, which I enjoyed a lot. But the main thing you do as a critic is try to ask yourself, "What's this about? What does it mean?" That's a hypothesis. It's like science. I mean you sort of abduct to an explanation of an artwork's existence, and you say if it means this, then that would make sense of this and this and this. And that would be to talk about embodiment. So it was a pretty good formula for doing art criticism, and the nice thing about it, ethically speaking, is that it postponed giving a judgment. By the time you found out what an artwork might mean and how it actually embodied the meaning, you got to like it, really. People say, "Oh, you're such a generous critic," but I really talked myself into liking things by finding out, as a matter of fact, what their anatomy was. That's the first thing I found out. The second thing I found out, after twenty-five years, was that I hadn't found a counterexample. That is to say, everything that was art turned out to be something that embodied its meaning, and I began to think rather well of *The Transfiguration*. I thought a book that held up for twenty-five years— no wonder they want to have a conference about it. Nothing has really changed since that time. Although the art world strikes most of us as a very tumultuous institution, from the philosophical perspective, nothing has changed. That's just the way I think it should be. Thanks very much.

2008

I'm Arthur Danto, and I have two métiers, you might say. I'm a philosopher, and in the last number of years also an art critic. I thought what I'd do this evening is to talk a little bit about how they're connected, at least in my case. Not that many people are likely to profit from this, because not that many people are going to find their lives joined up in quite that way, but I'll talk about philosophy in part because I think it's not a world that most people know very much about. People take a philosophy course or two, or even major in it, but to do it as a profession and to engage with other people doing philosophy has been an exceedingly rich experience. And then you find out that you're good at it or you're not good at it. Nobody knows at the age of sixteen or seventeen that they are a philosopher, let alone that it's something that they are likely to be good or mediocre at. You find out a lot about the kind of mind you've got by working at it.

The pivotal work connecting the two aspects of my life is a book I published in 1981 called *The Transfiguration of the Commonplace.* It's a philosophy of art, and I talked about it last year and also the year before at this time because it turned out that in 2006, the book was just twenty-five years old. It was enjoying a silver anniversary and there was a lot of discussion of it. There was an online conference, which I thought was pretty exciting as a way of relating to the entire community of people who would be interested in the kinds of questions that the book asks. *The Transfiguration of the Commonplace* can be seen either as the fourth volume of a five-volume work, or as the first volume of a three-volume work, depending on how you sort the books out. I was really lucky when I came up in philosophy, because I think I lived through a golden age. That is to say, there were an enormous number of extremely smart people doing philosophy in a novel way, in a way in which it had never been done before. I identified myself with what was, what is still called, analytical philosophy, which at the time was extremely optimistic. The thought was that you would be able basically to solve all the questions of philosophy by an analysis of language. There were schools of thought on which way language should be analyzed. One had the feeling that it was a golden age because discoveries were being made, discoveries of a kind that had never really been known about, though philosophy has a pretty long history in the West. This was extremely exciting. The idea was, in general, that if you're going to write philosophy—and there was no point being in it unless you were—you were going to present short, pointed papers to the community, and the only community that really mattered was the community of other philosophers who would read them and comment on them. The idea of writing books was considered somehow or other unwelcome. Nobody wanted to plow through books. People were willing to read these short papers. So for the first period in my life as a philosopher I did write a certain number of short, pointed papers, but I started to get the idea that I wanted to write a book, and I began.

It was kind of a discovery, I suppose, that there are certain kinds of sentences we use all the time when we're telling stories, narratives, and which make perfectly good sense in the past tense, but for one reason or another can't really be used in the present tense. For example—and they're almost like jokes—"The Thirty Years War began in 1618," which is pretty much boilerplate historiography. But, you couldn't have imagined somebody saying in 1618, "The Thirty Years War began today." That is to say, nobody knew that it really was a war, and nobody knew how long the war was going to last. Or "Petrarch opened the Renaissance." I mean, whatever Petrarch did to open the Renaissance, nobody knew at the time he did it that he was opening something that was going to be called the Renaissance. People can say that Erasmus was the greatest pre-Kantian moral thinker in Europe, but nobody could have said, "This is Erasmus, our preeminent pre-Kantian thinker," since Kant wasn't going to be born for three hundred years. So there are ways in which you can describe people retrospectively that you can't when using the sentence in the present tense. I call these narrative sentences because they relate two events, separated often by great distances in time, and where you use the later event to describe the first event, but at the time the first event takes place, you have no inkling as to what the future's going to bring. It's impossible to imagine having that kind of knowledge. I use as a really beautiful example a sentence in Yeats's poem *Leda and the Swan*, where Zeus incarnates himself as a swan and rapes Leda. Yeats writes, "A shudder in the loins engenders there / The broken wall, the burning roof and tower / And Agamemnon dead." It's an extraordinary line. If you were seeing an event like that—a woman being raped by a bird—it would be extraordinary in its own right, but you would have no sense that the entire future of the ancient world was being settled at that point. That is to say that Leda was going to become pregnant with Helen and Clytemnestra, the wives respectively of Menelaus and Agamemnon, and that Helen was going to be abducted by Paris, son of King Priam of Troy. That whole future was there, settled, so to speak, at that moment. But nobody was going to know that for years and years and years and years. And nobody could have said that line of poetry except in a poem looking back to that event.

The idea of narrative sentences opened up for me into a kind of fascinating study of the logical structure of the relationship between a narrative and an explanation. And before you knew it, I did have a fairly substantial book, which I presented under the title *Analytical Philosophy of History*. Once having that book out, I began to think that I would really like to write a lot of books, carrying forward not the philosophy of history, but the philosophy of representation that I had kind of discovered and worked out the logic of— a certain way of representing the world. It opened up the idea of thinking about representation as a central philosophical concept. It's easy to see how knowledge and action, for example, involve representations. You think basically that knowledge is a matter of getting representations to fit the world and that action is a matter of getting the world to fit our representations. So you've got two structures that are related, almost like mirror images. I was thinking fairly deeply about knowledge and action as together sharing a certain kind of structure, which was asymmetrical, going in one direction in one context and in a different direction in the other. I knew that at some point I was going to write a book about art because art played a very large role in my life.

I knew I was going to have to find some way of fitting art into this system that I saw myself as building. In 1964, I wrote an essay that was the kind of essay the profession looked favorably upon. It was called "The Artworld." I presented it for the American Philosophical Association at the annual meeting in December of 1964. It was unlike anything, I think, that had been written in the history of aesthetics, because it was about art of a kind that was different from anything that anybody would have known about in the long history of aesthetics. Aesthetic speculation began almost at the beginning of philosophy, in the writings of Plato, and there was a strong anti-artistic position taken by Plato and by his mentor, Socrates, followed by about twenty-five hundred years of animosity between philosophy and art, for whatever reason.

What interested me is this: When you began to look at what was happening in the art world in the 1960s, which was an extraordinary decade, you saw things that, if you were conversant in the history of philosophy, would at least have been amusing. In Book 10 of the *Republic,* Plato writes that there are three ways of thinking about the concept of bed: as a concept, as an article of furniture, and then as a representation—a picture of a bed. I noticed that there were beginning to be beds around the art world. That was really pretty humorous, as though the artists were commenting on a thought of Plato's. There was Rauschenberg's *Bed* [1955], for example, the bed on which he has a quilt and a sheet, and they're in a frame and he has slathered paint all over it. But you could sleep in it, *à la rigueur*. Oldenburg made a God-awful motel room [*Bed Ensemble*, 1963] with a bed that had white plastic sheets. George Segal had an actual cast iron bed in one of his installations. I thought, well, it's really interesting that after twenty-five hundred years the art world is changing, and artists are beginning to use real objects in their installations, and that they are beginning to make works of art that can't necessarily be easily told apart from real objects.

My favorite example of that was Andy Warhol's 1964 exhibition at the Stable Gallery which consisted in what Ric Burns, in his recent documentary [2006], described as grocery boxes. There were hundreds and hundreds of grocery boxes in that gallery. And the interesting question was, how do you know you're looking at a work of art and haven't just stumbled into a stockroom? There's a wonderful photograph of Andy standing between some of the *Brillo Box*es, pasty-faced, looking like a stock boy, photographed by Fred McDarrah for the *Village Voice*. Warhol had raised a question that had never been raised before in the form in which he did it. Philosophers certainly had asked, "What is art?"—I mean, that's a perfectly legitimate question. It's like what is oxygen or what is nutrition or something like that. But Warhol complicated the question in such a way that the answer was philosophically rich. His question was, given two objects which are indiscernible from each other, and one of which is a work of art and one is not, how do you tell the difference? In what does the difference consist, to put it in a somewhat different way? And I thought, that's the most interesting question I've seen raised about art by any philosophical writer, let alone an artist. At that point, my admiration for Warhol was without limits. I thought to have come up with that form of the question was an absolutely tremendous contribution to the philosophical understanding of art. And that, in a way, was what my paper "The Artworld" was about, but it was raised as a question because I didn't have an answer at that point. I had this idea that I was going to write a five-volume work on the theory of representation in different domains of philosophy and that when I reached volume four I would be ready to write about art and maybe would know what I was talking about.

But my romance with analytical philosophy cooled, and I wanted to write a different kind of book. The first three books were called *Analytical Philosophy of History, Analytical Philosophy of Knowledge, Analytical Philosophy of Action.* I didn't want to call this *Analytical Philosophy of Art.* I found this wonderful title, *The Transfiguration of the Commonplace,* in Muriel Spark's novel *The Prime of Miss Jean Brodie.* One of her characters has entered orders—she's a nun, Sister Helena of the Transfiguration—and she has written this book called *The Transfiguration of the Commonplace.* And I thought, that's just what I'm after. Absolutely perfect. What is the transfiguration of the commonplace? I thought that's what Warhol had done. He'd transfigured the tomato soup can. He'd transfigured the Brillo box. The notion of transfiguration itself is a religiously charged concept. And I thought that the *Brillo Box*/Brillo box problem was a lot like the Jesus/Schmesus problem, so to speak. That is to say, somebody looks just like Jesus, but Jesus happens not merely to look like this guy, but happens to be a god. And so you say they're indiscernible, so what is it that makes this one a god and this one just Schmesus, an ordinary guy in Jerusalem? They're indiscernible but the differences between them are momentous. One is a savior, et cetera, et cetera, and the other just, I don't know, pushes a wheelbarrow. The problem would be something like, here's the *Brillo Box* and it's a work of art, and here's a Brillo box and it isn't a work of art, so what do you have to add to that to get this? That's what *The Transfiguration of the Commonplace* was about.

The book's structure is that of a Socratic dialogue, in the sense that Plato depicts Socrates engaged in different searches. Usually the dialogues have a form of seeking a definition of some kind—the definition of justice in the *Republic*, the definition of knowledge in the *Theaetetus*, the definition of love in the *Symposium*. Somebody will offer a definition and then Socrates, who's very shrewd, will say, "Well, but what about this case?" and offer a counterexample. Then they say, "Oh well, that's tough, Socrates, but here's one way of meeting that counterexample." The dialogue proceeds like that. It's the classical way of writing philosophy: thesis, counterexample, then another, larger thesis that covers both, and then you keep going until you don't know how to find the next counterexample—you're not smart enough to find the next counterexample, and so you stop. *The Transfiguration of the Commonplace,* therefore, was in the nature of a search for a definition, in this case the definition of art. The definition is going to consist in a couple of necessary conditions. I never thought I could get beyond two conditions, but if I could find two necessary conditions I thought I would have made a lot of progress. I start offering a necessary condition, and then I look for some counterexamples, and I fight my way to the point where I think I've got that necessary condition nailed down, and then I pick up on a second necessary condition. It turns out that you've got a definition of art which is extremely impoverished, but it does seem to cover an awful lot of cases. I'm thinking first of all that a work of art has a meaning, it's about something. And secondly, that it embodies the meaning, in contrast with a proposition, which is about something where you've got some kind of grammar that relates the proposition to reality. Whereas the work of art embodies its meaning.

I thought in the end I had this definition. It was a pleasing definition. It was impoverished. I could imagine myself in China and saying, "I tell you, I've got a theory of art." And they say, "Tell me what it is." I say, "Well, a work of art is an embodied meaning." They say, "Oh well, let's see. That sounds interesting as a definition, but you're leaving out so much." And I say, "Well, I know I've left out a lot, but I'm not sure if what I've left out is really part of the definition of art. Maybe what I've left out is important for Sung watercolors, but I want a definition which is also going to cover Greek tragedy and is going to cover ballets and so forth. Each thing that I've left out maybe belongs to a given artistic tradition, but what I've got belongs to *every* work of art." That was the thesis that I thought the book contributed.

That idea of embodied meaning has been fairly useful. At least it's something you can get hold of and apply. And that brings me to the notion of art criticism. Because I found when I began to write art criticism that I was looking for meanings and how the meanings were embodied in the work. That is to say, in working out a piece of criticism it would be enough to describe the work—whatever it would be—in terms of what it is about and what meaning it has, and explain in some way how that meaning is embodied in the work. Then obviously, you're going to go a lot further than that in a piece of criticism, but it will give people a lot if you can manage to get across those ideas. Just as an example, recently there was an exhibition at the Metropolitan Museum of the paintings of Poussin. Poussin has never been an artist I loved. Richard Wollheim—now dead but a wonderful philosopher, and himself an art critic, although more conservative than I ever was—Richard adored Poussin. And I know other people who adore Poussin, but I didn't. I thought it was certainly a defect in me. But I was living with it and hoping that I could overcome it. I read a book by the art historian Tim Clark called *The Sight of Death.* It was about two Poussin paintings, *Landscape with a Man Killed by a Snake* and *Landscape with a Calm*, that just happened, by coincidence, to be at the Getty when Tim was there for a period of research. And he decided to look at those paintings for the six months that he was going to be there, look at them every day and keep a kind of diary. They asked me at *Artforum* if I would review the book, and I thought, well, I certainly don't know enough about Poussin to review the book, but I can at least see what Tim Clark thought was there. And I was really, really disappointed when I finished the book. I thought it wasn't worth writing a whole book like that. He didn't tell me enough that would justify writing at that length about just those two paintings. I got restless with that. But the Poussin exhibition came to New York and those two paintings were in it, so here was my chance to look at those paintings, and a great many others. I was particularly taken with a painting called *Blind Orion Searching for the Rising Sun*. There is a gigantic figure with a little tiny figure sitting on his shoulder. Orion has done something bad, and he's being punished by being made blind. It's at some cost that he's blind, I mean, it's a terrible deprivation. He's walking along and he's got his bow and arrow, which are of no use to him because he can't see. And he's got this little figure on his shoulders, and the little figure is guiding him toward the rising sun. The thought is that his blindness will be cured by the sun—at least that seems to be in the myth. So there was this intimate relationship between this figure on Orion's shoulders and Orion himself.

I thought, what is the meaning of this painting? What is it about? You can get the myth. You can see what the story's about, but—I had seen, just recently, an incredible piece by the British sculptor Antony Gormley at Sean Kelly's gallery—I guess you'd have to call it a sculpture—but it was a wide, round enclosure that you entered. Antony had constructed some kind of mechanism in which droplets of water filled the entire space. He called it *Blind Light*. When you got into that space you couldn't see your hands, you couldn't see your feet, you couldn't see where you were. I thought that there was a really interesting relationship between Antony's sculpture and Poussin's painting. I thought that Poussin's painting is about orientation. Also, I had been thinking a great deal about certain articles by Kant, on what is orientation in thinking, what is orientation in space. Kant makes a great deal of the fact that we're handed—that we have a left hand, a right hand, and we can orient ourselves. Then, is there anything analogous, Kant asks, in thought, anything that would orient us in thinking? He wrote about that off and on throughout his career, and I was very interested in that. So I had a third thing that I was able to connect to Poussin's painting. There was no historical connection, obviously, between any of them. But I thought about the concept of orientation and Antony's embodiment of the problem of orientation— that when you get in that space that you can't see, you have to orient yourself if you ever want to get out. I put that together with this painting of Orion, blind and looking for the sun. So I had some kind of structure, certain associations that I could bring to bear in describing that painting, and gave some flesh to the notion of meaning and to this larger idea of orienting oneself in the world. That is how I wrote about that particular work. And that is how I've been trying to write for most of my career as a critic, looking for what it's about and then where the embodiment is and then what larger thoughts I can attach to that.

There's just one thing more I would like to add, and then I'll stop. I've been fairly uninterested in what philosophers of an earlier period had to say about art. I thought I had the great fortune to live through a history that they didn't know anything about. They could have had no idea what the future of art was going to be like, living when Hegel did in the 1820s or when Kant did in the 1780s. Both of them wrote masterpieces—*The Critique of Judgment* by Kant, which is about art in a way, and the great lectures on aesthetics that Hegel delivered at the University of Berlin in the 1820s. Those are powerful books, but these great thinkers had no sense of where things were heading. What would they do if they saw contemporary art? How could they deal with it? How would they know it was art? Lately I've been thinking, is there some way in which they've got enough in those books so they could deal with it, if they should come back to earth? I saw a work by David Hammons at the L & M Gallery. It was kind of an ugly work. It was some old fur coats on coat stands. And he had damaged them. I think he had burned them and painted them. *Artforum* had two critics who were supposed to talk about the best works of the year. I guess it was 2007. Jack Bankowsky was one, and he thought this was one of the ten best, and the other critic thought the same thing. I wondered what Kant would have thought had he seen something like that, and somebody had said to him, "That's our art, Immanuel. This is what you've got to get used to if you're going to live in the twenty-first century." What would he say? I started going over a book that means a lot to me, *The Critique of Judgment*, looking for some things—and that book had meant a lot to the great critic Clement Greenberg, too. Greenberg thought that it was the greatest book ever written on aesthetics. He was not a philosopher, Clement, but he did believe that the best basis we have for aesthetics is Kant's *Critique of Judgment.* I didn't think that could be true. But I could see why that book would have appealed to Greenberg because it does talk about things—particularly the first part of the book—that are eighteenth-century concepts. The eighteenth century was when aesthetics as a body of thought had begun to emerge. It's about beauty and it's about taste. Beauty and taste—well, particularly taste—are concepts that have very little application today outside maybe interior decorating or choosing a dress. But taste has very little to do with criticism, very little to do with developing a critical attitude toward a body of art. Then as I went through the book I came across a thought that struck me as very profound. Kant has this idea that's quite surprising. He says, "You know, there can be a work that lacks nothing so far as beauty is concerned. And if somebody says, 'How do you like it?' I say, 'Well it's beautiful, all right.' And the person says, 'It sounds as though you've got reservations.' I say, 'I do have reservations. It lacks spirit.'" Kant uses this.

Some ways into the book he brings in this idea that you weren't prepared for, of spirit and of lacking spirit. How does he work that out, lacking spirit? He introduces a thought that he doesn't develop very far, but that seemed to me to be very impressive. He says that for spirit to be operative in the creation of a work of art, the artist has to have an aesthetical idea. It's an odd expression, the aesthetical idea, and in the eighteenth century it must have sounded strange indeed. An idea was something you were supposed to grasp mentally, through reason, but Kant calls it an aesthetical idea, which means we're supposed to grasp it through the senses. That's what aesthetics basically meant in Greek. So there has to be a sensory way of conveying an idea. I thought that was an interesting thought. He gives an example. He was never very rich with his examples, because he doesn't believe in examples, but this is a little bit striking. He says the eagle is the emblem of Zeus, so that if we see an eagle we say this represents Zeus. The eagle is shown with lightning bolts in his two claws. And you think to yourself, that is some powerful creature. He's able to hold lightning, lightning bolts, like sticks. Instead of just saying Zeus is powerful, you show this eagle holding these lightning bolts, and you have shown, through an aesthetical idea, the power of Zeus. That interested me because I thought, my God, Kant is talking about what I've been talking about. He's talking about embodied meanings. I wrote a piece recently which I called "Aesthetical Ideas as Embodied Meanings." And a friend of mine wrote an essay, the title of which was "Kant and Danto, Together at Last." And I felt really jubilant that I was able to connect that Kant had a rich enough idea that, if you worked at it, you could develop a theory of criticism and a kind of ontology of the concept of a work of art. Anyway, that's where I am right at this moment. So thanks.

2009

I'm Arthur Danto. I am a writer. The bulk of my writing has been in philosophy, but in the last couple of decades quite a bit of it has been about art. I more or less backed into the art world when I wrote a book on the philosophy of art, which got me an invitation to become an art critic, and so a lot of my writing over the last while has been in art criticism. When I've been up here in Maine, as a general rule, I'm working on some question of the relationship between philosophy and art, and I talk about that. But last summer I wrote a book for Yale on Andy Warhol, and they delivered a set of bound galleys to me the day before we were going to leave to come up here. I thought it would be kind of a hoot to do a reading, and I thought I would read the last chapter of the book, the title of which is "Religion and Common Experience"; it's about the place of religion in Andy's work. The book begins discussing a store window. It is Bonwit Teller, April 1961, and it's Andy's breakthrough show, it seems to me—it was his first show of paintings. Before that, he had shown ephemera, I guess you'd have to say, at places like Serendipity and various cafes, et cetera, et cetera. He was, as you know, an exceedingly successful commercial artist. A lot of his early work consisted of advertising illustrations of upscale shoes for women. His I. Miller drawings were admired even outside the world of commercial art, but in the main, they're entirely forgettable works. This is 1961, and he's broken through. A painting with the Pepsi-Cola sign, called *Advertisement*, he regarded as his first painting, and the German collector who acquired it for his collection, a Dr. Marx, felt that he had a great, great treasure there. I'll talk about some of these early paintings as I go along, because it seems to me that they do have a certain religious significance in their own right.

There were about five people doing work of this kind in New York around that time and most of them were at Leo Castelli's gallery. Andy bought a painting of a light bulb by Jasper Johns and asked if there was anything else he might be interested in, and Ivan Karp brought out a large painting of a girl by Roy Lichtenstein—it was based on an ad for an inn and a resort in Mount Airy, and Andy was shocked. He said, "I'm doing the same kind of work." Ivan was a bit astonished that in a matter of weeks he should have bumped into several individuals who didn't know one another but who were making art out of vernacular images. I was not in New York in 1961, I was in Europe, but had

I been, I don't know what I would have thought, had I passed the windows of Bonwit Teller. Andy's window wasn't up for very long—just one week. Would I have seen these paintings as art? What would my experience actually have been? I've speculated about that, but I've speculated even more about how Andy might have gone from an entirely trivial artist to somebody who was doing these extraordinary images.

Andy also painted an advertisement for plastic surgery and called it *Before and After*. He did it in several versions around that time, and I really do regard it as a masterpiece. I can see it in a photo of the Bonwit Teller window, behind a row of mannequins in dresses, as this kind of before and after that plays an immense role, it seems to me, in Andy's life. I think of Saint Paul, where he says, "When I was a child, I spake as a child, I thought as a child, I behaved as a child, but when I became a man, I put aside childish things." And here, I think Andy is saying, "I've put aside childish things. I am now really an artist." These early paintings are great enlargements of things that you would see at the back of blue-collar publications, advertising ways to get over what Grace Paley called "the little disturbances of mankind." When Andy's *Brillo Boxes* were shown at the Stable Gallery in 1964, it was the first time I really saw a possibility of thinking philosophically about art. But I'm not going to talk about that, since I've written about it extensively and also talked about it in several of my lectures here. What I'm going to do is begin with my current Warhol project, and I will read a fairly short chapter:

> Andy had, by nature, a philosophical mind. Many of his most important works are like answers to philosophical questions, or solutions to philosophical puzzles. Much of this is lost on many viewers of his work, since philosophy itself is not widely cultivated outside universities, but in truth most of the philosophical knowledge needed to appreciate Warhol's stunning contributions did not exist until he made the art in question. Much of modern aesthetics is more or less a response to Warhol's challenges, so in an important sense he really was doing philosophy by doing the art which made him famous. In other words, most of the philosophy written about art before Warhol

was of scant value in dealing with his work: philosophical writings could not have been written with art like his in mind, as such work simply did not exist before he created it. Warhol demonstrated by means of his *Brillo Box* the possibility that two things may appear outwardly the same and yet be not only different but momentously different. Its significance for the philosophy of art was that we can be in the presence of art without realizing it, wrongly expecting that its being art must make some immense *visual* difference. How many visitors to his second show at the Stable Gallery wondered if they had not mistaken the address and walked into a supermarket stockroom? How many, walking into a theater in which the film *Empire* was being shown, thought that they were looking at a still image from a film that had yet to begin its showing?

That happened to me. I went to see *Empire* at the Whitney, to see how much of it I could sit through, and a guy said to me, "When's the film going to show?" It had been on for twenty minutes, but it just looked like a slide, or a still projection.

Something similar can be true as well of certain religious objects, which we expect to look momentously different from ordinary things but which are disguised, one might say, by their ordinariness. Of the four vessels today claimed to be the Holy Grail, for example, the one that most persuades me that it might be genuine is an ordinary-looking vessel, drably colored, rather like an individual salad bowl, in a vitrine in the cathedral of Valencia in Spain. It really looks like something Jesus could have used at the table, given that he affected the life of the simple persons he lived among—carpenters and fishermen and the like. Of course, as befits so venerated an object, the *Sacra Cáliz*, as it is called, is supported by an ornate and gilded stand embellished with pearls and emeralds, but if one saw it by itself, it would be unprepossessingly plain, though it is carved out of a piece of stone. The Grail would not have been on so ornate and precious a stand at the Last Supper itself, where it was actually used for whatever was eaten on that tremendous occasion, touched with the lips or the fingers of who those present were certain was the Messiah.

I have to say straight off, I'm not a religious person at all, but I'm a little bit obsessed with religious concepts and find that they have a lot of application to art.

Jesus himself was like that bowl, if indeed, the claim is true that he was God in human form. Imagine that there was a man just his age in Jerusalem, who looked enough like Jesus that the two were often confused for one another, even by those who knew them well. The difference could not have been more momentous than that! Confusing a god with a mere human being is, *toutes proportions gardées*, like confusing a work of art with a mere real thing—a thing defined through its meaning with a thing defined through its use. Imagine a student who has followed a program of institutional critique whose thesis consists of substituting in a museum display an ordinary Brillo box for one of Andy's—a work worth $2 million at Christie's in exchange for a mere cardboard box of no greater value than that of the material of which it is made.

Relics are typically presented the way the *Sacra Cáliz* is in Valencia today—a fragment of bone is placed in a golden housing, set with priceless stones and perhaps images of the saint, to whom the bone is believed to have belonged. One has to take it on faith that the bone is the bearer of special powers, but in the nature of the case it must look like a mere human remnant, and be able to pass all the obvious tests, like DNA assay. It is felt that the Grail must have extraordinary powers, given the belief that it was touched by God incarnate, but the history ascribed to the Grail, if it really still exists, has left no traces on its surfaces. That it was touched by Christ's lips, that it held Christ's blood, cannot be deduced from anything the eye now sees. Its plainness alone testifies to the possibility that it was present at the last meal Christ shared with his disciples, where it looked like an ordinary dish, maybe a little special given the special character of he who used it. But the test for whether Jesus was God embodied is not part of the forensic repertoire. The Transfiguration described in the Synoptic Gospels was intended to show selected disciples that Jesus transcended the merely human, for example, by his radiance. But the so-called Messianic Secret was meant to be kept quiet—Jesus preferred not to be trooped after by groupies thirsting for miracles. For anyone other than witnesses to the Transfiguration, Jesus was out and out human.

I respond deeply to a description of Christ's humanity by the great art critic Roger Fry in regards to a painting by Mantegna, now in Berlin: "The wizened face, the creased and crumpled flesh of a newborn babe . . . all the penalty, the humiliation, almost the squalor attendant upon being 'made flesh' are marked." To paint God incarnate, the Christian artist need paint only a human being. Of course there were external indications, like halos, that represented the other aspect. But these would be mere symbols, the way gold frames symbolize that they protect works of art. Bleeding is evidence of being human, but there is no such simple evidence of divinity.

I have plunged into certain religious matters because of a thought of the philosopher Hegel, who said that philosophy, art, and religion are what he called "moments" of Absolute Spirit. I offer this because it suggests that art, philosophy, and religion are forms through which human beings represent what it means to be human. One of the things that is distinctive of human beings is that the question of what it is to be human arises for us in a way that it doesn't for other animals. There is, in that respect at least, an analogy between artworks and religious objects, and that may be a way to approach the question of whether and in what way Warhol's art actually is religious. What is undeniable, of course, is that he was a Catholic, whose mother was quite pious, and that he and his mother prayed together, at home and in church. After her death he continued to attend Mass. In truth, most of those who frequented the Silver Factory were born and raised Catholics, including most of the Mole People.

The Mole People were out-and-out druggies who formed in the sub-population of the Silver Factory. If you saw *Chelsea Girls* you'd see, for example, Ondine going into a tantrum, and he was kind of the leader of the Mole People, as they called themselves.

The critic Eleanor Heartney, herself Catholic, has written a very searching study, *Postmodern Heretics*, in which she describes "The Catholic Imagination in Contemporary Art," to use her subtitle. A great deal of the content of contemporary art in America involves aspects of the human body that imply Catholic attitudes, but these aspects at the same time are offensive to a conservative Catholic morality. A good example is Andres Serrano's incendiary *Piss Christ*, in which a plastic crucifix is displayed in a container of the artist's urine. This caused an immense uproar when it was exhibited in the Richmond, Virginia, Museum of Art. Serrano is Catholic, and it is not difficult to see that he was vividly depicting the way in which Christ was "despised and rejected," to quote Handel's *Messiah*—jeered, spat upon, and hit. Pissing on someone is conspicuously humiliating and degrading. Urine and spit are heavily laden with contempt, as feces or vomit would be, or menses. In my view, Serrano was seeking to restore the way Jesus was humiliated as he carried the cross to Golgotha. To be sure, it was a plastic effigy—but what difference does that make? Is the crucifix not an object of worship as much so as the person crucified? When Barnett Newman, a Jew, painted the Stations of the Cross, he did so in a very abstract and what one might call interior way. It is about unendurable pain, fainting, and giving up the ghost. But it offends no one the way Serrano's piece certainly does. Years ago, I quoted one of Yeats's "Crazy Jane" poems to a member of the so-called Moral Majority when we were both on a panel charged to discuss the National Endowment for the Arts and the highly sexual work of the photographer Robert Mapplethorpe: "Love has pitched his mansion in the place of excrement." He replied that it was hardly Yeats's finest line, and I asked him to quote me a finer one. Crazy Jane was one of Yeats's inspired inventions for addressing the sexed body and the physical basis of human love.

Warhol did not particularly like to be touched, especially by women, according to Viva, but he certainly had a kind of gleeful curiosity about sex and sexual parts, and made a point of showing it in his art, especially in his movies. Whether this can be explained by his Catholicism is hard to say. But nothing more sharply distinguishes the art of the 1950s from that of the 1960s in New York than the difference in how death and sex are represented in the two decades. Robert Motherwell—a Protestant—painted the great series of abstract canvases under the title "Elegy to the Spanish Republic." Serrano showed cadavers in a morgue. De Kooning's great paintings of women in 1952 were daringly misogynist, with their heavy breasts and bared teeth. Mapplethorpe photographed huge penises, or fists pushed into assholes. The fact that painting gave way to photography in the 1970s has to be crucial in how the same subject would be addressed. Andy tried to exhibit drawings of nude boys at the Tanager Gallery on Tenth Street, where they were rejected on principle, though Andy's drawings were never as robust as his silkscreens. Abstraction can, as easily as not, be understood as a form of repression, which can then make Pop seem itself a form of liberation. But the sexual revolution of the 1960s was bound to show up in art as well as life, without this necessarily meaning that the artists whose work took on sexual content were especially Catholic. It was a change in the culture. Most of the facts affecting Andy's religiousness belong to his biography. But none of this shows that Warhol was especially religious in his art.

Let us consider his last substantial body of paintings, based on Leonardo's *The Last Supper*, which are thought by some to be evidence of Andy Warhol's religiousness. As so often happened in Warhol's work, the idea came from elsewhere, in this case from the dealer Alexandre

Iolas, who had a gallery in Milan. Andy was one of five painters Iolas selected to do paintings based on Leonardo's *The Last Supper*. His idea was that a show of Last Suppers by contemporary artists would generate interest, since the gallery was across the piazza from where Leonardo's masterpiece was undergoing its latest restorations, and there would have been an incentive for visitors to take in both it and versions of it by painters of our day. Warhol specialists have observed that he found the reproductions of *The Last Supper* in art books too dark, explaining why he used cheap copies of the old painting instead. But in my view, what is important about the fact that the original is Leonardo is that *everyone knows Leonardo's painting*—it belongs to the common consciousness of the culture that Warhol shared with everyone who knew his work, and which he took as his artistic mission to raise to self-awareness—to show our inner life to ourselves. Leonardo's *The Last Supper* is one of the few paintings that enjoys this status—Warhol's can of Campbell's tomato soup is another— though few of those who know *The Last Supper* ever actually saw it in Milan; it is better known through its many reproductions. To show *The Last Supper* as commonplace is to show it as it appears on a postcard, the way Duchamp showed the *Mona Lisa*, or in a calendar of masterpieces. Ask people to name ten paintings, they will inevitably name *The Last Supper*, not *La Conversation* of Matisse, let alone *The Last Sacrament of Saint Jerome* by Domenichino or one of the Mont Sainte-Victoire landscapes by Cézanne.

They probably wouldn't make the list. I don't know if there are ten paintings that everybody knows, but if they know any, they know *The Last Supper* and they know the Campbell's soup cans.

Andy treated the Last Supper as he treated many of his subjects. He did versions that showed series of the *Last Suppers*, much like his serial paintings of soup cans or dollar bills. He doubled Jesus, the way he doubled Marilyn, or Elvis. Repetition was a sign of significance.

But if you show Jesus twice, that's a little like showing that he had a double meaning or a double identity—that's at least my view. But he did the same with others.

He filled it with logos from contemporary products, like Dove soap, to represent the Holy Spirit, or the Wise owl from the familiar potato chip package, emblematizing wisdom. Or he used the General Electric logo to emblematize light. All these came from the commercial world in which he and the rest of us are at home, though it is fair to say that none of them held religious significance as such. Warhol's great artistic project began with the images in the Bonwit Teller window and evolved on two levels—the level of fears and agonies, and the level of beauties. The level of plane crashes, suicides, accidents, executions; and the level of Marilyn, Liz, Jackie, Elvis, Jesus, radiant with glamour and celebrity. A dark world with radiant beings, whose presence among us is redemptive, and into whose company Warhol sought to insinuate his own ungainly presence, and to make stars of us all. His mission was to externalize the interiority of our shared world. *The Last Supper* has penetrated the common consciousness with the momentousness of its message. In making it his, he too has become part of what we are. And by making it his he shows us that it is ours, part of life, rather than something one has to travel to Italy to see—in this respect it is like the dish sometimes held to be the Grail, commonplace rather than rare, a dish like any other rather than something crusted with jewels and made of precious metals. Or, like his own early prints, something that one could buy for a few dollars at the receptionist's counter at Castelli's, where they were displayed in stacks. A genuine work of art for five bucks!

His first show at Castelli's was a show of the four flowers, and they were five dollars apiece and you could just roll one up and pay your five dollars and walk out. I thought that would be a nice thing to hang in my younger daughter's room—she was just a baby. But they're rare now because people who paid five dollars for them didn't think they were important enough to preserve.

No wonder he stenciled low price tags—like $6.99—on pictures of masterpieces.

The painting that most clearly alludes to the hiddenness of religious truth is perhaps Warhol's *Camouflage Last Supper*, where the visual message of the painting is distorted by an overlay of visual noise. Warhol began to use camouflage in 1986, the same year in which he did his *Last Suppers*, and used it as well in connection with his own self-portrait, in which it carries something like the same meaning it does in *Camouflage Last Supper*: it reveals the hiddenness of his own truth, which is all on the surface. He famously said, "If you want to know all about Andy Warhol, just look at the surface: of my paintings and films and me, and there I am. There's nothing behind it." He even did a series of works consisting of nothing but camouflage, which as a visual pattern had become as ordinary and as everyday as violence itself in the modern world, however unusual its appearance in art—as unusual as *Brillo Boxes* in art galleries would have been in 1964, for that matter. Critics saw the camouflage works as ready-made abstractions, but what they mean is that their subject is completely hidden. The camouflage swatch has in fact become the portrait of the political reality of our time, too horrifying to look upon directly. The inference, on seeing someone wearing camouflage, that it is a soldier, is based on a social truth that camouflage is the visible mark of the military in our time.

My feeling is that the hiddenness implied by camouflage belongs with the idea that confidences were disclosed at the Last Supper. What meaning could be more secret than that the wine and bread are Christ's flesh and blood, and that in partaking of these Jesus becomes part of the blood and flesh of the partakers? But I do not think Warhol became a religious artist in the last years of his life, with *The Last Supper* paintings.

I think the religious turn, if there was one, happened much earlier. I believe that at some moment between 1959 and 1961 Andy Warhol underwent an artistic change deep enough to bear comparison with a religious conversion—too deep, one might say, not to be a religious conversion. Before then, his work had a certain effete charm, consisting of plump cherubs, posies, pink and blue butterflies, pussycats in confectionery colors. He made a handsome living as a commercial artist, whose chief product consisted of playfully erotic advertisements for upscale ladies' footwear. My feeling is that his religious identity was disclosed in April 1961, in his first exhibition—installed, symbolically, in a site displaying soft fluttery summery resort wear for the class of women for whom the luxurious shoes that had given him his first success were designed—the windows of Bonwit Teller, one of the great emporia for upscale women's clothing on Fifth Avenue in New York. Warhol, as we saw, surrounded the mannequins with blowups of the coarse, grainy advertisements one sees in the back pages of cheap newsprint blue-collar publications. The images he appropriated after the conversion were vernacular, familiar, and anonymous. They typically advertise cures. A montage of black-and-white newspaper ads is for falling hair; for acquiring strong arms and broad shoulders; for nose reshaping; for prosthetic aids for rupture; for love elixir ("Make him want you"); and for Pepsi-Cola ("No Finer Drink"). It projects a vision of human beings as deficient and as needy. It was a message not unlike that of Joseph Beuys, whose symbols were fat and felt, to minister to the hungry and the cold. All religion is based on suffering and its radical relief. It was as if the message of saviors had been translated into the universal language of cheap American advertisements. The Bonwit Teller show testifies to what remains perhaps the most mysterious transformation in the history of artistic creativity, Warhol's "before and after."

In a great photograph of Warhol's studio taken by Evelyn Hofer just after his death there is a large painting, on the far wall, a double portrait of Jesus presiding at the Last Supper, his eyes cast down, while two disciples, Thomas and James, gesture with great animation to his left. In that studio photograph, many other paintings are shown, leaning against the side walls. The only other picture that faces us, however, shows a bowl of chicken noodle soup blazoned on the familiar red and white Campbell's soup label, with the familiar logo, the neatly written *Campbell's*. The image on the label is of a mass-produced china dish, whose utterly commonplace decorated rim rings the Queen of Soups like a halo. I find it affecting that the two images—*Campbell's Soup Can* and *Last Supper*—mark the beginning and the end of Warhol's career—at least, once he found his way. But I find it no less affecting that the plate on the label echoes the plate on the table at which Jesus appears to be gazing with his downcast eyes, as if the plate embodies some profound meaning. I imagine Warhol standing before the two paintings, at the final moment he was to spend in his studio, looking at both the dishes as if they were cognate Grails.

What his final thought as an artist was, of course, is impossible to say, but I like to think that it has to have been about two dishes, one empty, the other full of our daily soup, warm, hot, filling, tasty, like the answer to a prayer. The two paintings together reveal his calling as an artist. He is *grateful* for the daily bread asked for in the Lord's Prayer.

That's more or less something Roy Lichtenstein told me, "Isn't this a wonderful world we live in?" He said Andy said that all the time.

Meanwhile, he was in terrible pain from the gallstones, for which he knew and feared that he would soon require an operation. The trip to Milan for the "Last Supper" show had been physically agonizing. The second and last death struck him on February 22, 1987, at New York Hospital.

When I say the second death, he was legally dead when Valerie Solanas shot him in 1968. The second bullet ricocheted off bones and touched something like seven vital organs that are in there. You could tell the extent of the damage by the scars, if you have seen Alice Neel's painting of him semi-nude, or Richard Avedon's photo of his bare torso. Anyhow, Mario Amaya, who had been at the studio to discuss an exhibition with Andy, and also was shot, was taken to the hospital with him. Andy had been declared dead. According at least to legend, Mario said, "Do something, he's Andy Warhol. He's rich." And they massaged the heart and brought him back to life. He wasn't dead that long, but he was dead, and if he hadn't been Andy Warhol, he might have been permanently dead. All that meant something to him. He thought a lot about having died for the rest of his life.

He died peacefully and to the surprise of everyone.

Thank you.

Arthur C. Danto

Arthur C. Danto (1924–2013) was born in Ann Arbor, Michigan. He spent his childhood in Detroit, and enrolled in Wayne University (now Wayne State University) to study art and art history after spending two years in the Army. He attended graduate school at Columbia University in New York City.

From 1949 to 1950 Danto studied in Paris with Maurice Merleau-Ponty on a Fulbright scholarship. In 1951 he returned to New York to complete his Ph.D. and teach philosophy at Columbia, where he subsequently became Johnsonian Professor of Philosophy. Upon his retirement in 1992 he was named Johnsonian Professor Emeritus. He was the recipient of many grants and fellowships, including two Guggenheims and a fellowship from the American Council of Learned Societies. During his career as a philosopher, he served as vice president and president of the American Philosophical Association and president of the American Society for Aesthetics. From 1984 until 2009 he was the art critic for *The Nation*. He was married to the artist Barbara Westman.

He is the author of many books on philosophical subjects, including *Nietzsche as Philosopher* (1965), *Analytical Philosophy of Action* (1973), *The Transfiguration of the Commonplace* (1981), and *Narration and Knowledge* (1985). He also published many books on art criticism, including *Encounters and Reflections: Art in the Historical Present* (1990), which won the National Book Critics Circle Award for Criticism; *Beyond the Brillo Box: The Visual Arts in Post-Historical Perspective* (1992); *After the End of Art* (1997); *The Abuse of Beauty* (2003); *Andy Warhol* (2010); and *What Art Is* (2013).

The Acadia Summer Arts Program

The Acadia Summer Arts Program—commonly referred to as A.S.A.P., Kippy's Kamp Kamp Kippy—is an internationally known summer artists' residency located near the breathtaking Acadia National Park, on Mount Desert Island, Maine. Since 1993 the program has furnished invitees with the time, space and resources to rejuvenate their creative practices. Each year, A.S.A.P. convenes an impressive array of artists and arts professionals, including museum directors, curators, critics, architects, painters, sculptors, filmmakers, musicians, poets, dancers, art historians and others. The island is dotted with A.S.A.P.'s private cottages, which guests are free to use as either peaceful work space or for simple rest and relaxation. Most of the guests' time is unstructured, but the program provides weekly communal activities—dinners, guest lectures, and boat excursions to the surrounding islands—and annual events such as exhibitions, film screenings, dance performances and concerts.

Marion "Kippy" Boulton Stroud, the founder of A.S.A.P., has had a lifelong passion for supporting and facilitating artistic production. In 1977 she founded the Fabric Workshop and Museum in Philadelphia, where she currently serves as artistic director. Having spent summers on Mount Desert Island since childhood, Kippy wanted to share the beautiful Maine landscape with her friends and colleagues. Beginning as a small gathering in Kippy's coastal home, Shore Cottage, the program has blossomed into a summer-long influx of more than three hundred guests each year. Consequently, the physical space has evolved into a complex of studios, offices and lecture facilities, designed by Robert Venturi, Denise Scott Brown, and the late Steven Izenour of Venturi, Scott Brown and Associates. Despite this growth, the intimate, familial quality of A.S.A.P. remains.

Published by Acadia Summer Arts Program

Publisher: Marion Boulton Stroud
Producer and Designer: Takaaki Matsumoto/Matsumoto Incorporated, New York
Manager of Publications: Amy S. Wilkins/Matsumoto Incorporated, New York
Editors: Elizabeth C. Baker and Amy S. Wilkins/Matsumoto Incorporated, New York

Printed and bound by Nissha Printing Co., Ltd., Kyoto, Japan

Text by Arthur Danto
Copyright © 2014 by Acadia Summer Arts Program
All text by Arthur Danto © Arthur Danto
"Pieces of Thought: Arthur Danto at A.S.A.P." © Marion Boulton Stroud
All images courtesy of Acadia Summer Arts Program

Library of Congress Control Number: 2013948895
ISBN: 978-0-9797642-6-4

Available through D.A.P./Distributed Art Publishers
155 Sixth Avenue, 2nd Floor, New York, New York 10013
Tel: (212) 627.1999 Fax: (212) 627.9484
www.artbook.com